THE SECRET BOOK OF SPY HUMOR
VOLUME TWO

The Secret Book of Intelligence Community Humor

ALSO BY THE AUTHOR

Stories from Langley: A Glimpse Inside the CIA

Briefing for the Boardroom and the Situation Room: A Brief Guidebook

The Counterintelligence Chronology:
Spying by and Against the United States from the 1700s Through 2014

The Secret Book of CIA Humor

Two Spies Walk Into a Bar

Coaching Winning Model United Nations Teams

Food with Thought: The Wit and Wisdom of Chinese Fortune Cookies

The 50 Worst Terrorist Attacks

Terrorism Worldwide, 2017

Terrorism Worldwide, 2016

Terrorism 2013-2015: A Worldwide Chronology

Terrorism, 2008-2012: A Worldwide Chronology

Terrorism, 2005-2007: A Chronology

Terrorism, 2002-2004: A Chronology

Terrorism, 1996-2001: A Chronology

Terrorism, 1988-1991: A Chronology

International Terrorism in the 1980s: A Chronology of Events 1984-1987

International Terrorism in the 1980's: A Chronology of Events, 1980-1983

Transnational Terrorism: A Chronology of Events, 1968-1979

The Literature of Terrorism: A Selectively Annotated Bibliography

THE SECRET BOOK OF SPY HUMOR
// VOLUME TWO //

THE SECRET BOOK OF INTELLIGENCE COMMUNITY HUMOR

//  //

EDWARD MICKOLUS

WANDERING WOODS PUBLISHERS

The Secret Book of Intelligence Community Humor

By Edward F. Mickolus, PhD

Copyright © 2018 by Edward Mickolus

All rights reserved. No part of this publication may be reproduced, stored in a retrieval system, or transmitted, in any form, or by means electronic, photocopy or recording without the prior written permission of the publisher, except in brief quotations in written reviews.

First Edition May 2018

ISBN-13: 978-1-949173-00-0

Published in the United States by Wandering Woods Publishers

Book Design, Cover and Typesetting by
Cynthia J. Kwitchoff (CJKCREATIVE.COM)

ABOUT THE AUTHOR

Edward F. Mickolus, PhD served a 33-year career with the Central Intelligence Agency in analytical, operational, management, and staff positions in four Directorates. His work at the CIA included analysis of international terrorism and African politics, covert action, HUMINT collection, counterintelligence, public affairs, and recruitment. He is a recipient of the CIA Career Intelligence and the Clandestine Service Medals.

Dr. Mickolus has written over 30 books, teaches courses on intelligence tradecraft, and is the President of Vinyard Software whose International Terrorism Data Center provides the best publicly-available data on terrorists and events around the world. He received his PhD in Political Science at Yale University.

A recovering standup comic, he often gives presentations on his collection of 1,000 fashion-challenged neckties and collects classic automobiles.

ACKNOWLEDGMENTS

Thanks go to Randy Tauss, Barbara Dean, Susan Simmons, Michael Douglas Smith, Steve Richter, David Cariens, Greg Kmiecik, David Chizum, Ben Cates, Clint Mesle, Jon Hittle, Christopher (sorry, we're protecting his last name. He knows who he is.), Kurt, Timmy W.-Y-, Emil Levine, Brian G., Becky S., Dan K., the Association of Former Intelligence Officers, the CIA Retirees Association, and a host of colleagues who chose to remain anonymous, some because they're still under cover, some because they don't want their colleagues knowing that they were responsible for these practical jokes and thereby engage in retribution (which will be chronicled in volume 3 of this series!). Thanks also to ace proofreader Tim Lightfield and the always brilliant Cindy Kwitchoff.

DISCLAIMER

All statements of fact, opinion, or analysis expressed are those of the author and do not reflect the official positions or views of the CIA, the Office of the Director of National Intelligence, any other Intelligence Community organization, or any other US Government agency. Nothing in the contents should be construed as asserting or implying US Government authentication of information or Agency or ODNI endorsement of the author's views. This material has been reviewed by the CIA and Office of the Director of National Intelligence to prevent the disclosure of classified information. This wasn't the toughest review for the PRB, which once had to review a tattoo—the author did not say when it would be shown—and a gravesite.

TABLE OF CONTENTS

Introduction	1
Return of the Pranksters	3
After Hours	15
Travels With the DCIs	17
More Family Ties	19
Puns	22
Analyzing the Russians and Others	27
The DIA Analysist	38
A Visit to NSA	59
As if the Director Doesn't Have Enough to Worry About	74
For Sale, Aston Martin, Slightly Used	81
Whatever Happened to Shaken, Not Stirred?	86
Dress Codes	89
Engagement Codes	97
DI Stylin'	100
The Editors Strike Back	108
DO Stylin'	120
Notes from the CIA's In-Box	137
Office of the DNI	148
Be Careful Where You Turn	161
Guide to the Denizens of the IC Family	165
Training	169
What the Support Folks Have to Deal With	172
An Early Brush With Fame	179

INTRODUCTION

To publicize the first volume of *The Secret Book of CIA Humor*, the International Spy Museum and the Riot Act comedy club in Washington, DC, were kind enough to host a standup performance of the book's highlights. Among the material I used in the routine:

- It's an honor to work for the 2nd greatest intelligence service in the world. The best, of course, is AARP. When you turn 50, no matter where you are, they'll find you. I think that's how the Agency finally found bin Laden—they contracted it out to AARP. By the way, battling CIA for 2nd spot are the people who track down those delinquent on their student loans.

- I've been casting for *Spying With the Stars*, a new reality show. Each week a celebrity will have an espionage-related challenge. Lady Gaga will run a surveillance team, trying to blend in with the crowd. Snooki will try to hold her liquor against the Russian team at a cocktail party. And Simon Cowell will try to recruit someone by pretending to be a nice guy.

- Although the Agency strongly supports improving one's language capabilities, I've never been particularly adept at learning languages (although my Klingon is still pretty good). I was in a class for 3 weeks before it dawned on me that no one actually speaks Manganese.

I also used the "you might be a Taliban if…" Since the publication of the book, a mid-level Taliban commander contributed another indicator: Mohammad Ashan, suspected of plotting two attacks on Afghan security forces, appeared at an Afghan police checkpoint in Paktika province, carrying a wanted poster displaying his face. He requested the $100 finder's fee, insisting," yes, yes, that's me! Can I get my reward now?" So if you find your name on a wanted poster in Afghanistan, and try to claim the reward…

This book includes a few CIA-specific stories, pranks, and other forms of humor, but expands beyond the first volume to include humor from across the 17 members of the Intelligence Community. You'll soon see that the humor of these organizations reflects their unique organizational cultures, and sometimes subcultures.

As was the case with the earlier volume, this book is a compilation of contributions from a host of friends across the Intelligence Community. I've rewritten them in first-person to give it a consistent "voice," but rest assured that I'm not this clever to have instituted all of these pranks by myself.

There are also numerous one-liners on intelligence and fictional intelligence characters from the Internet. So if you wrote:

James Bond: Waiter, there's a fly in my soup.

Waiter: No, sir, that's actually a bug.

thank you for your anonymous contribution.

And for your protection, in case of fire, please exit the building before tweeting about it.

RETURN OF THE PRANKSTERS

In the first volume of *The Secret Book of CIA Humor*, we revealed the old Shout Your Badge Number Down the Burn Chute prank. Corridor radio has wised up the rookies to this joke, so their seasoned colleagues have had to develop new techniques. The latest: New urinals in the men's rooms feature motion detectors that automatically flush the urinal when the user steps away from the porcelain facility. Rookies are told to swipe their badge against the detector, because the Agency is conducting drug testing and we need to have a record of whose urine is being collected.

// ⊕ //

The first volume also mentioned that rookie photo analysts were directed to go to the supply room for cloud eradicator. An enterprising young National Geospatial Intelligence Agency employee discovered that such a product—by that name—could be found on the Internet. It is used on car windows to eliminate fog.

// ⊕ //

An advertisement that appeared in the Crystal City metro stop, sponsored by ClearanceJobs.com: Real Analysts Do It in a SCIF. (*Ed's Note:* Secure Compartmented Information Facility.)

// ⊕ //

Most denizens of the four directorates agree: they are simply united by a common janitorial service.

// ⊕ //

When I was between wives, I tried to learn how to cook. I had a recipe for cookies and thought I'd treat my office to my latest learning adventure. I was missing one ingredient and thought "baking powder, baking soda, they're both involved with baking, what's the difference?" and substituted the ingredient I had for that which I lacked. My office was appreciative of the effort but asked that I try something else to show my solidarity with the team.

// ⊕ //

And then there was The Great Tuna Fish caper. An officer bragged to everyone in his circle of friends and colleagues that he was on a new high protein weight-loss diet. Every day he brought in a can of tuna fish and a box of soda crackers. At lunch break, he would open the can, spread the tuna on a cracker and wolf it down. It became a ritual for months. He bought cheap cans of tuna, and they had the old-style pasted on labels. Eventually, he brought in a dozen or so cans of the stuff and stored it on a filing cabinet adjacent to his desk. Someone bought a can of cat food with tuna innards in it, removed the cat food label and replaced it with a tuna fish label. The altered can was then surreptitiously inserted into his stack of tuna fish cans when he wasn't around. The can was carefully inserted a few levels down in the stack. The switch was virtually imperceptible. (This was an early example of a CIA tech modification operation.) The guys kept track of where the modified can was in the stack, and finally the day arrived and everyone was lurking around to see if he would notice. He opened the can of cat food, inserted a spoon, spread the muck on a cracker and took a bite. "Ugh! Must be spoiled!" he cried. The jig was up, as the laughing and snickering broke out around him, but for years he has claimed he immediately knew a switch had been made....but that remains in doubt.

// ⊕ //

During a very sensitive initiative in support of the DO, a small team of DI imagery analysts were put on a 24-hour surge schedule. They were working night and day over their light tables to meet a critical deadline, and they were reporting directly to our then-Office Director, Wayne. One of these guys, a senior analyst named Bob, had worked so hard over so many days that sometime during the graveyard shift at 3 or 4 AM, he put his head down on his light table and just conked out. When the rest of the guys in the branch started showing up around 6:30, Bob was sound asleep, snoring away there at his light table. Ever so gently, the guys lifted the big orange nylon light-table cover up and dropped it over Bob's head and upper torso. So now Bob is covered from the waist up, hunched over a table and just blissfully snoozing away. Then the guys took a pink office message memo and wrote: "BOB—COME AND SEE ME IMMEDIATELY! —WAYNE." Eventually, Bob woke up under his tent, found the ominous note and was rushing down the hallway sweating bullets to report to the front office before the guys headed him off.

// ⊕ //

I worked in a facility like a lot of government buildings, whose offices and cubicles were constructed of removable aluminum wall studs, making it fairly simple for the contractors to come in and move a wall from here to there, open up a space, create a new space, and so forth. Remove a few bolts, move the stud over, slap on some sheet-rock, prime and paint. Voila! Government office. There was some extensive remodeling underway on the floor above ours. When a branch chief up on that floor took leave for a 2-week vacation, a cabal of mischievous employees talked the contractors into removing the door to the branch chief's office and replacing it with a (temporary) plain wall matching the rest of the wall in that long corridor. When the branch chief returned from vacation, he couldn't find his office, walked up and down looking for the door. It likely crossed his mind that he was in the wrong vault on the wrong floor, until he heard the laughing and snickering.

// ⊕ //

Photocopy of handwritten sign, located outside of women's washroom:

> Lost:
> Sense of Innocence and Wonder.
> Last seen Shrunken, Whimpering, and Cowering
> If found, please call x55555.

Note: The extension noted above directs one to CIA's Office of Public Affairs. (*Ed's note:* I once had that phone line. Oddly enough, it was the same extension on The Hill given to Elizabeth Ray, referred to in a book as the Washington Fringe Benefit. The subject of a major Congressional sex scandal, she was a comely secretary whose resume did not include typing skills.)

// ⊕ //

When I was a young DI analyst, I coached a softball team named FNU LNU, named after a famous unknown individual, First Name Unknown, Last Name Unknown. We got a lot of second looks from folks in law enforcement, who use the same nomenclature. Rookie analysts would always ask their wizened mentors (the term didn't exist back then, but you know what I mean) who this "FNU LNU guy is that I'm reading so much about. He seems to get around a lot." "Yes," the wizened one would say, "he's one of our top agents. You wouldn't believe his travel bills."

// ⊕ //

I was a young intern working in a small, unwindowed interior office with three other young officers. One day, the Office Director wandered in and decided that we needed artwork on our walls to help improve our morale. We filled out the forms to get some wall hangings. Logistics sent over three trapezoidal structures. One evening, I snuck them out of our office (thereby improving the look of our place) and into the neighboring corridor. I tacked them up and printed onto a note card "From Squantum to Hull," by a famous artist (who shall go unnamed here). After awhile, I noticed that the note card was missing and worried that Security was on to me. Surely they were doing some special forensic investigation and would find my fingerprints, or DNA, or something on the note card. I was quite relieved the next day to discover that an aluminum plaque had been placed beneath Squantum. Later that summer, a brass plaque replaced the temporary aluminum one. I was never found out, but I did find out that art is truly in the eye of the beholder.

// ⊕ //

One day during lunch, I made a $20 bet with my cafeteria colleagues that we could get people to respond to messages we wrote on a dollar bill. I wrote "If found, please address to X", a P.O. box I had created for the operation. Six weeks later, a high school kid sent me a postcard saying, "I have your $1 bill, but how do I know that you'll reimburse me?"

I sent the kid a note just saying "trust me". The kid did, because the bill arrived. I won the bet and sent her my winnings, a tidy profit of $19 for her. I worry now that perhaps I made her too trusting of strangers, and something bad has come of her. Meanwhile, one day I was called up to the Director's office, where I was met by the chief of Security, among others. Showing me another one of my marked dollar bills, they said, "you're not in trouble. We just want to know whether this is part of some top secret Agency operation." When I assured them that it was not, they said that although this was not illegal, they would appreciate my not doing this anymore, because the action could become a fad and result in people hoarding dollar bills. Thus ended a great practical joke.

// ⊕ //

I was quite proud of my brand new (to me) white Mercedes and didn't want it to get door dings in West Lot, the parking lot seemingly many miles from the Headquarters back entrance. So I tacked a note onto the For Sale bulletin board offering to pay $100/month to any senior official who would rent me their indoor parking spot in the Director's garage. I later got a call from the Director's special assistant, who counseled me, "Do you want a spot in the Director's garage? Work hard, get promoted, and one day you, too, will be able to park there. We don't rent out these spots."

Speaking of the Director's garage, a friend rushed into the office of Executive Director Buzzy Krongard lamenting that he had seen a (fictitious) crash in the garage of a visitor's car into that of Buzzy's Bentley Brooklands.

// ⊕ //

One of our rookie analysts was particularly proud of his self-described command of the English language and would merrily argue over happy/glad editorial choices. Having had enough of this unproductive use of his and our time, we approached the PDB briefer of a senior who received his product. The briefer wrote a note on the side of one of the analyst's articles complaining about the analyst's word choice, reporting that the principal was very upset with his work.

// ⊕ //

A rookie who had just become a father was subjected to a sporadic parade of us, offering well-wishes for his fictitious new assignment—a 3-month detailing to a site far from home that would require him to sleep in a cot at his desk for the entire time, away from his family. We kept this up for a few days before telling him the truth.

// ⊕ //

When I was head of the DI training branch in the Office of Training and Education, OTE's director became so enraged during a staff meeting that he jumped on the conference table and began screaming at people. Shortly after that, logistics came through and painted all the interiors. On the top floor, where the director's office was located, they painted all the doors pink. I posted a sign by the elevator reading: "Pink is used in insane asylums to calm criminally violent inmates."

Logistics also decided to add more color, so they put up large canvases painted in complementary colors to the door. On our floor the color was purple. They put up a lavender canvas (about 4x4). I printed a small card that read: "Sunrise at Ballston" Gary C. $400.00"

// ⊕ //

My favorite blog posting: "I will be out of the office for a few days on vacation. I've scheduled a post to automatically update every morning, so hopefully the fun times will continue even in my absence. But just in case the automatic updating doesn't work—I'll be back next Wednesday and will return to regularly daily posting at that time. If I'm not back next Wednesday, please avenge my death."

// ⊕ //

Our OTE Director and I existed in a continual state of war. One year he sponsored a Christmas door contest. So, I did a series of pen and ink drawings based on the Far Side. One was a snake sitting in a chair bloated from having had a big meal. A female snake was standing in the door. I had her saying, "Director, how many times do I have to tell you not to fill up on branch chiefs and then go to the Christmas party!" I also did one that showed a female insect inside a woman's hair do. The insect was on the phone saying: "Gladys? This is Sylvia. I have just moved into my new digs at Mary Ann's in time for the holidays." I forget the rest. At any rate, a number of SOVA analysts sent me congratulatory emails, and several rode the shuttle to Ballston to see the door. We did not win the prize.

Analysts never enjoyed putting together the Current Intelligence Reporting List (CIRLs). One summer day, the East Europe branch in the DI decided to get them out of the way. The head of the Bulgarian party and government, Todor Zhivkov, had a dragon-lady daughter named Ludmyla. As a joke, our Bulgarian analyst wrote the following: "Ludmyla Zivkova, an apolitical nymphomaniac, in a turnaround, is rumored to be power hungry. Please report on…" The sentence made it through all the review process and editing and went world-wide. Our analyst thought someone would see the humor and take it out.

In the realm of analysts having to use their ability to think on their feet outside work, the following happened to me. Janice has a brother (Dick) who is 18 years older; she is very protective of him. When Dick was 80, he needed hand and wrist surgery for carpal-tunnel syndrome. So we went to Cooperstown, NY to help out. The day of the surgery, Janice decided to drive. I was under strict instructions to take Dick into reception and get him signed in, while she parked the car. No problem, right? We get there, and Janice drops us off at the door. Dick and I walk up to the reception's desk, and in a voice that could be heard all over the lobby he announces, "I'm here to see the main hand-job guy." The face of the receptionist turned bright red, and she could hardly contain herself. As a good analyst, I had to say something, so I blurted out, "We don't let him out of the basement very often." With that the whole lobby broke in laughter—just as Janice is walking through the door. She walks up to me and says, "What did you do, now?"

My friend Gary thwarted my masterpiece. I found a full-page picture of a doctor of veterinary medicine with his right arm up a horse's ass all the way to his arm pit. I was going to post it with a sign saying," DI management at work." I made the mistake of showing it to Gary (the definition of wimp). The next day it had disappeared from my desk.

A DI analyst phoned the Watergate –on an Agency phone—at the height of the Watergate crisis, identified herself as an Agency employee, and asked for a copy of the complex blueprints.

// 🌐 //

My friend Bob had a high school buddy who was convinced that he was a spy and always gave him a hard time. On a business trip, Bob stopped by his home town to pay a visit to the high school buddy. Bob filled a briefcase with random papers, mostly newspapers, locked it, and drove a quarter mile from the buddy's house. He sprinted to the house with the briefcase (so that he was all sweaty by the time he arrived), banged on the door, and when his buddy answered the door, thrust the briefcase into his hands and said something along the lines of "Hide this in a safe place! Never open it and don't tell anybody that you have it!" He then sprinted away, going back to his car and into another story.

// 🌐 //

An Intelligence Community historian offered this observation on a specific date in history: The first meeting of the US House of Representatives occurred on March 4, 1789. At that time, they called the roll and realized that they did not have enough for a quorum. The end of the day's notes state: *But a quorum of the whole number not being present, the House adjourned until tomorrow morning at eleven o'clock.* That line appeared every day for the next four weeks. And which day did they finally have a quorum, meaning the day they actually began conducting business? April 1, 1789. Which is also April Fool's Day. Coincidence? You decide.

// 🌐 //

The Navy is the home to some of the greatest anachronisms, which in turn lend themselves to pranks. There is an art form to "salting" your language with naval terms from the age of wooden ships and iron men. We don't mend sails any more, but we still have "rope yarn" days for training. Even ashore—doors are hatches, floors are decks, and the stairs are ladders. Navy Chiefs (E7-E9) are the ultimate keepers of Navy lore in the Chief's "Goat Locker". Were there ever goats there? Probably a hundred years ago! A great game to play with new sailors and officers in the Navy is to send them on a Snipe Hunt (wild goose chase) throughout the ship in search of things like relative bearing grease, left-handed wrenches, and of course, mail buoys. By the way, phones on Navy ships are "sound powered", but that's another story.

// ⊕ //

On Soviet Navy Day, allied Naval Intelligence officers around the world met locally for the Red Tie luncheon, in which officers wear a red tie fashioned after the Soviet naval ensign. (I still have mine!) The lunch always ended with the toast, with water, "To the Soviet Navy. Bottoms Up!" The annual Day is still celebrated, but the toast has been changed whenever the Russian naval attaché staff attends.

// ⊕ //

The Navy Field Operational Intelligence Office (NFOIO), housed at NSA, featured aviator Lt. Bobby Mansfield, who was not thrilled with being an analyst. When called upon to brief senior Pentagon officials, he began, "Good afternoon admirals, gentlemen: the classification of this briefing is TOP SECRET OGLETHORPE. Is anyone here cleared for OGLETHORPE?" When no one admitted to having this clearance, he closed his black notebook (which contained only blank paper) and walked out. Mansfield had invented OGLETHORPE, which would have a long-lasting heritage. Several months later a senior NFOIO analyst working with Mansfield was phoned by a CIA analyst doing an all-source study on Soviet surface-to-air-missiles. He asked if NFOIO had any OGLETHORPE information on the subject. The senior analyst said he was surprised that CIA knew the Navy codeword, noted that OGLETHORPE did not contain such material, and asked the CIA to not use the codeword again. The senior analyst also reports that the KGB asked spies Robert Hanssen of the FBI and Aldrich Ames of CIA "What is OGLETHORPE?" and that debriefers asked KGB defector Vasili Mitrokhin "What is OGLETHORPE?"

// ⊕ //

During a visit to the NFOIO analysts' "Snake Pit" by a senior British official, a Lieutenant Commander scissored off the necktie of a briefer. After a few minutes into the briefing, the briefer returned the favor, cutting the Lt. Commander's tie. The briefing ended, the slack-jawed guest left, and the duo walked to a filing cabinet and retrieved new ties from the hundreds collected from the Salvation Army.

// ⊕ //

When the US Drug Enforcement Administration was created in 1973, several personnel joined from the CIA. Most rarely referred to their former employment, but Sid (an alias) constantly spoke of his time with "Mother," reminding everyone that Mother could call you back anytime. About once a month I would leave a US Government yellow message form in his basket, stating in badly scribbled handwriting, "Sid. Call immediately. Urgent." with the phone number 703-351 (CIA exchange) and two or three of the next four numbers smudged. Sid would spend the next several hours asking everyone on the floor stating "Mother called me. It is urgent," and asking if they took the message and what were the numbers. It never failed until he retired many years later.

// ⊕ //

Fed up with whining, one Army denizen created DA Form IMT WF1, dated April 2009, the "Hurt Feelings Report", which appears below:

Hurt Feelings Report

For use of this form, See FM 22-102;
the proponent agency is TRADOC
Data required by the Privacy Act of 1974

Authority: 5 USC 301, Departmental Regulations; 10 USC 3013, Secretary of the Army and E.O. 9397 (SSN)

Principal Purpose: To assist whiners in documenting hurt feelings, and to provide leaders with a list of soldiers who require additional counseling, NCO leadership, and extra duty

Routine Uses: For subordinate leader development IAW FM 22-102. Leaders and whiners should use this form as necessary

Disclosure: Disclosure is voluntary, but repeated disclosure may result in a DA Form 779-1A, Report of Wall to Wall Counseling

Part I: Administrative Data
   A. Whiner's Name (Last, First, MI)
   B. Rank/Grade
   C. Social Security Number
   D. Date of Report
   E. Organization
   F. Name and Title of the Person Filling Out This Report

Part II: Incident Report
   A. Date Feelings Were Hurt
   B. Time of Hurtfulness
   C. Location of Hurtful Incident
   D. NCO or Officer Sympathetic to Whiner
   E. Name of Real Man/Woman Who Hurt Your Sensitive Feelings
   F. Rank/Grade
   G. Organization (if different from 1e above)
   H. Injury (Mark all that apply)
      1. Which ear were the words of hurtfulness spoken into?
         Left   Right   Both
      2. Is there permanent feeling damage?   Yes   No   Maybe
      3. Did you require a "tissue" for tears?   Yes   No   Multiple
      4. Has this resulted in a traumatic brain injury?   Yes   No   Maybe
   F. Reason for Filing This Report (Mark all that apply)
      - I am thin skinned
      - I am a wimp
      - I have woman/man-like hormones
      - I am a crybaby
      - I want my mommy
      - The Army needs to fix my problems
      - My feelings are easily hurt
      - I didn't sign up for this
      - I was told that I am not a hero
      - The weather is too cold
      - Two beers is not enough
      - My hands should be in my pockets

- I was not offered a post brief
- Someone requested a post brief
- All of the above and more

H. Narrative (tell us in your own sissy words how your feelings were hurt)

Part III: Authentication
a. Printed name of real man/woman
b. Signature
c. Printed name of whiner
d. Signature

We, as the Army, take hurt feelings seriously. If you don't have someone who can give you a hug and make things all better, please let us know, and we will promptly dispatch a "hugger" to you ASAP. In the event we are unable to find a "hugger", we will notify the fire department and request that they send fire personnel to your location. If you are in need of supplemental support, upon written request, we will make every reasonable effort to provide you with a "blankey", a "binky" and/or a bottle if you so desire.

DA FORM IMT WF1, APRIL 2009   EDITION OF APRIL 1989 IS OBSOLETE

AFTER HOURS

I was intentionally working late one evening in the 1980s to put finishing touches on material I was presenting in a class the next day. I knew the Agency's computer system was "going down" for maintenance at 7:00 PM, so I worked diligently against the clock. All of a sudden at 6:45, the system went down without warning. I immediately called the Agency's computer office and was told it had been taken down for maintenance. I complained that the official announcement said the system would be taken offline at 7:00. I demanded that it be put "back up" so I could finish my work. It was, and I finished for the night and left the building. On the way home, what had transpired hit me, and I began laughing out loud. I, then a GS-09 or 10, had just demanded and caused the CIA to put its computer system back online until the appointed hour so I could finish my work! I later learned that this incident was quite a subject of interest at staff meetings the following day.

There are always tensions between the central managerial complex of an organization and its field representatives. That Headquarters-Station tension is known in CIA as the International Idiot Line. Draw a meridian somewhere between the US and whatever region you find the field representatives. (Sometimes this is the International Date Line, which lets us tell this story in this section!) No matter what side of that meridian you're on, the guys on the other side are idiots.

Being an avid (crazed?) runner throughout much of my career, no thunderstorm was going to stop me! I was running just outside the Headquarters compound after work one evening, right under a torrid lightning storm. Knowing that an uncle had been struck and killed by lightning as a boy, of course I understood the danger. But I wanted to get my run in without resorting to the track inside. Hearing a terrible crashing crack over my head, I looked up and saw a streak of lightning traveling down a power line—in my direction. Running faster, I looked again and saw the streak heading down a pole. Looking back once more, I saw the streak on the ground with an intent that was unmistakable—it was after me! Needless to say, my feet began to fly, much faster than ever before. I thought I was pretty fast, but who can outrun lightning? It struck me on the foot. Terrified, I ran back to the building and collapsed, thinking "Thank God for rubber soles." I reported the following day, saying I was electrified and energized for work! This was another incident that made it to high-level staff meetings.

// ⊕ //

That must have been a year for thunderstorms, for not long after being struck by lightning, a severe storm again came upon Headquarters around 5:00 one evening as I was preparing to leave for the day. When I got to the door and saw how bad the storm was, this time I wisely opted to wait it out. I sat down on the bench by the guard's desk and let the guard know why I was waiting there. After I had waited patiently for quite some time, the guard without prompting got on his phone and summoned a security vehicle to pick me up and deliver me to my car!

TRAVELS WITH DCIs

DCI William Casey addressed the Edward Weintal Prize Ceremony at Georgetown University on April 13, 1983, telling the assembled journalists, "When I was asked to address you on my views about journalism, I thought it an unusual opportunity for a Director of Central Intelligence. I am reminded of a Shogun in old Japan who was riding across his kingdom when he came upon one of his samurai, bloodied and woe-begotten. The Shogun asked him what had happened. 'My Lord, I am just back from doing battle with your enemies to the East,' answered the warrior. To which the Shogun replied, 'But I have no enemies to the East.' The Samurai paused and then said, 'You do now!' As I look around the world today, I am certain I don't need any more adversaries. My objective here tonight is not to create any new ones."

// ⊕ //

John Helgerson, in his *CIA Briefings of Presidential Candidates, 1952-1992*, recounts the December 22, 1991 meeting with President-elect Clinton and his just-announced national security team. Little Rock airport had become fogged in and none of them could fly out on schedule. They all went to dinner together, except for one—DCI-designate R. James Woolsey. The assembled worthies had joked that "those CIA folks" must have spirited the new boss away to some clandestine location. Helgerson reveals that a CIA communications officer on the Agency transition team rented a car on Woolsey's dime and drove him hundreds of miles to Dallas so that he could catch an early morning flight to an important meeting in California. Like the postal service, neither wind, storm, sleet, fog nor a socked-in airport will stop the Agency from completing its mission.

MORE FAMILY TIES

How does one tell one's child that you work in intelligence? I have a 7-year-old daughter who is a typical 7-year-old (must…tell…everyone…what…I…know). I did my best to explain things in "kid" terms without going into detail. She was so confused that my husband finally told her that I'm the Tooth Fairy. I'm going to have a lot of explaining to do when she gets older.

// ⊕ //

Many years ago I worked Family Day at the CIA. The guy in the office next to me made a sign to look just like the other door signs, but this one said "Roswell Alien Cryogenic Storage Facility". He put it over his office door for the day. I remember walking out of my office to see a 10-year-old kid standing and staring at that sign, and then running down the hall yelling at the top of his lungs, "Mommy! Daddy! It's here! It's here! I told you so! I told you so!"

// ⊕ //

When I was a new hire as a military analyst in the DI, the guys in my unit—including my very first Branch Chief—invited me to join their slow-pitch softball team. I accepted. We played after work at East Potomac Park against other Agency and DIA teams. My younger brother was in town visiting me that spring and I invited him to a game. My Branch Chief's spouse frequently showed up as did some of the other spouses.

During the course of the game, I introduced my brother to my Branch Chief—and to his spouse, who was from New Jersey and, frankly, a bit of a ditz. So as the game progressed and we came in for our turn at bat, I noticed my brother standing next to my Branch Chief's wife over behind the backstop. I walked over just in time to hear this exchange:

WIFE TO LITTLE BROTHER: "So where are you from?"

LITTLE BROTHER: "I am from Iowa."

WIFE TO LITTLE BROTHER: "Oh wow! Idaho! What do you do there?"

LITTLE BROTHER: "No. Iowa, not Idaho....."

WIFE TO LITTLE BROTHER: "Oh yeah, Ohio! I have never been out west."

LITTLE BROTHER: "Not Ohio. Iowa."

WIFE TO LITTLE BROTHER: "Oh wow! So what do you do way out there in Iowa?"

LITTLE BROTHER: "I am a school teacher."

WIFE TO LITTLE BROTHER: "Oh wow! A school teacher, huh?"

LITTLE BROTHER: "That's right."

WIFE TO LITTLE BROTHER: So, like....I mean, what is there to do out in Iowa? I mean, what do you do for fun?"

LITTLE BROTHER: "Well, I love to play golf. I play quite a lot of golf."

WIFE TO LITTLE BROTHER: Oh wow! I play golf, too. Do you mean they ACTUALLY play golf out there in Iowa?"

LITTLE BROTHER (running out of patience): "Yeahhhh....we manage to get in a few rounds between Indian attacks!"

WIFE TO LITTLE BROTHER: [Speechless. Apparently trying to figure out if he is pulling her leg.]

Conversation ended. At that moment I was certain my career in CIA was over before it even got started. But my Branch Chief never mentioned it nor did he hold it against me in any way.

PUNS

Ed's note: This collective attack by punsters from across the Intelligence Community is not for the faint of heart. If you have any difficulty swallowing puns, please turn to the next section of this book. For those of you who like puns, and you know who you are, you unfortunate oppressed minority, herewith, the Intellipedia coverage of Snackistan:

Snackistan

ABBREVIATION:	SNK
MOTTO:	Let's go out to the kitchen. Let's go out to the kitchen. Let's go out to the kitchen and have ourselves a snack.

Location Information
COUNTRY:	Snackistan

Staff Information
FOUNDER:	Ayatollah Granola
LEADER:	King Bing (AKA "King Don," AKA "Ding Dong", AKA "Ding Dong Il")
OTHER LEADERS:	Kim Jong MyTummyHurts (Supreme Taste Tester)

Snackistan is the mythical land of milk and honey—Milk Duds and Bit O'Honey, that is. Citizens are known as Snackistanis or sometimes, Snackers. The highest point in Snackistan is Mountain Dew at 15,000 feet above sea level. The lowest point is Sugarcrash swamp at 150 feet below sea level.

The most common mode of transportation in Snackistan is via Yumvee, with more prominent government members traveling via Stay-Puft aircraft and Blacklicorice birds. The "Bird Squadron" is under the command of Lord Switzer "The Twizzler" Licorice, a German Immigrant to Snackistan.

Snakistani Symbolism

There is an ongoing effort to discover more information related to the use of symbols in Snackistani culture. For instance, like the Bald Eagle in America, there is great reverence for the Honeybadger in Snackistan because it "takes what it wants".

Government Agencies
- National Sweets Agency (NSA) is responsible for SWEETINT collection; its ambassador is MaryJane Wegrzyn.
- The Department of Desserts (DoD) is responsible for securing and mobilizing all sweets, with Nicholas Hatfield as the attaché.
- The Natural Snacks Intelligence Center (NASIC) is subordinate to the DoD, responsible for reporting on foreign snack technology and mobilization.
- The Candy Intelligence Agency (CIA) is responsible for YUMINT collection.
- The National Goodies-Intelligence Agency (NGA) is responsible for IMINT collection, to include Snack Aperture Radar (SAR) requirements.
- The Doublemint Intelligence Agency (DIA) is responsible for collection at the State Department level. J.F. Wrigley, Director.

- The Department of Homemade Snacks (DHS) is responsible for domestic counter(top) intelligence. The Director is Dr. Oscar Mayer.
- The Open Snacks Center (OSC) is responsible for fresh and timely distribution of information on publicly available snack sources.
- The NutRageous Office (NRO) – (OOOMPA LUOMPA//EVERLASTING GOBSTOPPERS) is filled with "Non-Analysts" who build, launch, and operate the "Ridges Satellite Chips" and bring the highest technology improvements to the Golden Ticket Chocolate Bars for the US. It is rumored that these items are followed by Atomic Fireballs at End-of-Snack.
- The Fudge Baker's Institution (FBI) is responsible for developing and deploying the latest in chewy and gooey snacks in order to combat Domestic Hunger Attacks. The Director is Mr. Nestle N. Hersey.

The National Health official is Dr. Pepper, who is currently being housed in a secure facility at an undisclosed chilled location for protection, according to YUMINT reporting.

Snackistan currently has two entities located outside of the country. The Snackistani Outpost is currently located at a National Sweets Agency-established SCIF, though its exact location is subcompartmented FIZZY to protect the identity of the forward-deployed in the area. It is currently under command of Snackistani Gravy Commander Stuffing. The Snackistani Embassy is currently located at NSAW and is staffed by a CST (Candy Support Team).

The Snackistani Gravy (SNKG) currently has the SGV (Snackistani Gravey Vessel) STOVETOP patrolling the Big Red Sea.

Insurgency

Snackistan is currently under attack from an insurgent group known as the Insulin Insurgency, led by a powerful man, Bazooka Joe. The group is provided spiritual leadership by Wali al-Wonka, a prominent figure who earned his title at Candyland University. Flip flops on the ground provided Candy Intelligence (CI) which indicates al-Wonka is being sheltered by a secretive group known only as the Adults in Candyhar, and is currently out of reach of the Snackistani authorities. Notorious terrorist duo Ben & Jerry have been seen near Candyhar, and Operation Gobstopper has been launched to determine their activities.

The Insulin Insurgency has known connections to the IBC in Ireland, led by Mr. Pibb. It is not established if they have contact with known terrorists Baskini Rob'bins or Hage N. Daas. The Spiritual home of the II is the city of Haribo.

The Insulin Insurgency have been known to use Pop Rocks & Soda IEDs, as well as Mento-and-Coke mortars, as well as Fanta 110A/(G)rape, /(O)range and the Fanta Lite6Pak mod 1.

Reliable YUMINT reporting indicates that the Fanta Like6Pak mod 1 was purchased from the Sodastinian group known as HUMMUS in late June or early July 2011.

SWEETINT shows indications that the Insurgency engineers, funded by the mysterious Payday (also known as the 100 Granders) group believed to be operating out of Candyhar, have begun design on the FantaLike6Pak mod 2 (codenamed BUBBLES) to include a dousing range of 350 km.

All-source reporting indicates that the Insulin Insurgency has acquired Atomic Fireball technology from the Curds and intends to use its Warheads on the Sour Patch Kids or local Jolly Ranchers.

The Insulin Insurgency has claimed the capture of the Snackistani capital, and a major Snackistani leader, Col. Laffy K. Taffy, has fled. The actual ate of Col. K. Taffy is undetermined.

Department of Dessert reporting indicates chatter of a new weapon codenamed: Crybaby. This is also referred to as "Tear Jerker". The weapon is known to support an optional Warhead attachment. This configuration is being called the "Air Head".

New Reporting: Indications that the Mars Incorporated Liberation Front (MILF) is planning low level attacks against consumers in Fritolaysia.

Gummi Bear Battle: The Gummi Bear Battle is regarded as the most violent offensive action yet taken by the Insulin Insurgency.

Published by the National Goodies Intelligence Agency

References

Collection on Snackistan, the Insulin Insurgency, and all related persons of interest is very limited. Please contribute if you happen to collect any cereal reports on these entities!

Ed's note: Haven't had enough? Here's one final pun treat:

SPOILER ALERT: Gratuitous Barbara Frietchie Pun Follows

Former Deputy Director for Operations Clair George was known for the following shaggy dog story:

A KGB officer, getting his instructions from his branch chief before going out to his new posting, was told that all that mattered was recruiting a CIA officer. Nothing else would do. A CIA officer, being assigned to the same country, was told that he must recruit a KGB officer and that other recruitments didn't matter.

The duo showed up to their assignments, and eventually they ran across each other at a cocktail party. They did the usual social dancing around each other, sniffing out each other's interests, hobbies, and potential vulnerabilities.

Eventually they discovered that they shared a deep, dark, hidden secret—they were both gay. They fell in love with each other and agreed to sham recruitments of the other. CIA and KGB management was pleased and promoted the duo. For years, they passed each other corridor gossip from their respective agencies, keeping up interest in the operations, but not spilling any damaging secrets.

After several years, KGB and CIA counterintelligence agents caught on to their duplicity and set a trap. The duo met for a last tryst in their favorite hotel room. When the KGB and CIA counterintelligence teams jointly broke down the hotel room doors, they found the duo in flagrante in bed. The KGB officer boldly sat up and admonished the CIA officers: "Shoot, if you must, this old grey Red, but spare your country's fag."

ANALYZING THE RUSSIANS, AND OTHERS

The US Air Force and the KGB agreed to decide a victor in the Cold War by a simple dog fight. Two years hence, they would bring in one dog for a no-holds barred dogfight, winner take all. The Soviets secured the biggest, baddest dog from Lubyanka prison and mated it with a Siberian wolf. Feeling confidence in their steed, they sauntered in to the area of combat. The Air Force showed up with an 8-foot long dachshund. The Soviet's dog immediately began snarling and approached the dachshund, certain that the contest would be done soon. Suddenly the front half of the dachshund opened up, baring rows of teeth, clamped down on the wolfhound, and swallowed it with one gulp. The aghast Soviets asked what kind of dog it was. "Well, while you were breedin' that wolfhound, we were figuring out how to make an alligator look like a dog."

// ⊕ //

A Soviet and an American were sitting on a Moscow park bench, arguing about who had the better country. The American said, "My country has freedom of speech. In fact, I can walk right up to the gates of the White House and shout, 'Reagan is an idiot!' and no one will arrest me."

The Russian responded, "well, in the Soviet Union we have freedom of speech, too. In fact, I can walk right up to the Kremlin gate and shout, 'Reagan is an idiot!' and no one will arrest me!"

// ⊕ //

A Soviet diplomat was waiting to see the British Foreign Minister when he struck up a conversation with one of his British counterparts about which system was better: Soviet communism or Western capitalism. When asked about his salary, the British diplomat said, "I cannot discuss my pay with you, but I can tell you that I do very well. In fact, I do so well that I have 3 cars. When I go to work, I drive the Mercedes. When I visit my friends, I take the BMW. And when I go to Europe, I drive the Porsche. How about you Soviet chaps?" The Soviet diplomat responded, "Well, of course, I also cannot talk about salary, but I can tell you that Soviet government provides all transportation. When I go to work, I take Metro. When I go to see friends, I take bus. And when I go to Europe, I drive the tank."

// ⊕ //

(*Ed's note:* Here's a longer version of a joke that ran in *The Secret Book of CIA Humor*. Let me know which version you prefer)

The Louvre announced that it was planning to open a new art exhibit featuring a long-lost painting by Rembrandt of Adam and Eve in the Garden of Eden. The French government decided to invite all foreign diplomatic missions to a preview of the painting before opening it to the public. The Foreign Minister of France, as host, received the honor of viewing the painting first. He remarked to his aides, "See how Adam looks at Eve with such passion in his eyes? Adam and Eve must have been French!" Afterward, the British ambassador to France came in, viewed the painting, and remarked to his aides, "What noble features! What regal bearing! Adam and Eve must have been British!" Finally, the Soviet ambassador to Paris came in, viewed the painting, and remarked to his aides, "They are naked, homeless, have only an apple to eat between the two of them, and they think it's Paradise. Adam and Eve must have been Soviet!"

// ⊕ //

Putin is having dinner at a high-class restaurant with Medvedev, Shavalov, Zubkov, and others. "What will you have, Premier?" asks the waiter. "I'll have the steak," Putin says. "Vegetables?" the waiter continues. "They'll have the steak, too."

// ⊕ //

A new prisoner shows up at the Gulag. He tells his new Gulag-mates that he got a 25-year sentence of hard labor. His new Gulag-mates ask him what crime he committed in order to get 25 years. "Nothing!" he exclaims. "I am innocent!" "That's ridiculous," says one of them. "The innocent get only 10 years."

// ⊕ //

Two Moscow militia were assigned to guard an area at 10 p.m. A curfew had been placed on city residents, and the guards were given strict shoot-to-kill orders for any curfew violators after 10 p.m. The streets began to empty the closer it got to 10 p.m. At 9:55 p.m., a man was seen running out from an alley between the two buildings, straight across the park. The first militia member checked his watch and saw it was 9:55. The second militia member also checked his watch and saw it was 9:55. He looked up for a second, then raised his rifle and fired, felling the running man. The first looked at him and said, "I know we have a shoot to kill order, but curfew doesn't begin until 10. It's only 9:55. Why did you shoot him?" The second replied, "I know where he lives. He would not have made it."

// ⊕ //

In the early days of collective farming, a local commissar was on his way to visit a local kholkhoz. A local farmer greeted the commissar and said, "Good day, comrade commissar! Come to check on the crops?" "Good day, comrade farmer, I have! How are the potatoes?" "Oh, comrade commissar, the potato crop is so excellent, that if we stacked them they would reach the feet of God!" "But comrade farmer, of course you must know there is no God!" "Yes, comrade commissar, but there are no potatoes, either."

// ⊕ //

A Moscovite finally saved enough to buy a shiny new Lada auto. He waited in line to place an order. When he finally reached the front of the line, he proudly slapped down his pile of rubles and proclaimed that he would like to buy a Lada. Knowing that his color choice was either black or black, he said "I do not care what color it is." The official, after stamping 14 different forms, replied, "Thank you, comrade! Your car will be delivered exactly one year from today!" The Moscovite replied, "Morning or afternoon?" The official, with a look of confusion, came back "It is a year from now! What difference could it possibly make?" The Moscovite simply replied, "The plumber is coming in the morning to fix my water."

// ⊕ //

Under capitalism, man exploits his fellow man. Under communism, it's the other way around.

// ⊕ //

A Soviet soldier walks into a Moscow bar and orders two single shots of vodka. The bartender says, "Why not order a double? It's cheaper." The soldier replies, "My buddy shipped out to Afghanistan, so I'm drinking one for me, and one for him until he returns." The bartender pours him two singles. After several weeks, the soldier returns, obviously in emotional distress, and orders a single shot of vodka. The bartender says, "Oh, no! Did something happen to your buddy in Afghanistan?" The soldier says, "No, the doctor ordered ME to stop drinking!"

// ⊕ //

In a salute to David Letterman's Top Ten, Directorate of Intelligence Russia-watchers circulated the following:

Top Five Indicators Russia's Attempts to Woo Europe Succeeded
1. "I'm with Putin" t-shirts are best sellers at Milan Fashion Week
2. McDonald's France Happy Meals feature turnip burger with side of borscht, milk-flavored vodka
3. Male life expectancy in Hungary drops to 32
4. Belarus, Abkhazia replace UK, France on UN Security Council
5. Poland invites A.Q. Khan over for tea

Not to be outdone, an analyst mimicked the DI writing style to produce a more detailed analysis of these activities:

Russia: Attempts to Woo Europe Are Awkward, Creepy

Russia is hitting on Europe using a combination of suggestive innuendo, aggressive flirting, and a heavy dose of machismo, making Europe feel uncomfortable and weird. We assess Russia's amorous efforts are reducing the effectiveness of the UN because most of Europe hid in the bathroom and smoked during the last General Assembly meeting to avoid meeting Russia.

- Russia claims that Europe is so hot just being in the same room is enough to cause a premature ICBM launch, according to mutual friends. The URL of Russia's mission to the EU has also been changed to www.silovikilikeitsinful.com.
- Russia believes that when they say no, they mean yes, according to Chechnya, who should know.
- Yevgeny Primakov frequently parks outside 10 Downing Street with binoculars and a notebook at odd hours, with the windows frequently steamed up, according to British security services.

Russia's charm offensive is meeting little success, we judge, and Russia's flaky friends Iran and China aren't helping. Russian "wingman" Ahmadinejad's leering glance suggests he's imagining Europe naked every time they meet. His small, beady eyes set too close together stimulate unpleasant memories of Europe's uncle who liked children too much and had to go away.

- Whenever Australia tries to talk to Europe about Russia, Europe tries to change the subject to something "more cheerful," like global warming, according to Australia's MySpace page.
- China has difficulty accepting breakups and believes "fresh blood and lives" are a good way to get back together. This is kind of a turn off, according to Taiwan.
- Europe found Russia's abuse of 98-pound weakling Georgia brutish and unattractive, according to emotional intelligence, with the exception of Finland and Germany, who were secretly impressed by the size of Russia's BMPs. (*Ed's note:* infantry fighting vehicles.)

The social disruption of Russia's lame moves is causing a number of relationship rethinks around the globe. In a low probability, high impact scenario, Pakistan is considering whether it has been too boring and the US will pay more attention if it acts "more crazy," according to India.

- Turkey is a little confused about whether Russia likes her or not in that way, and is thinking of losing some weight, possibly North Cyprus, just in case, according to Turkey's cousin Turkmenistan.
- Canada has confided that, seeing Russia's behavior, it really appreciates the US a lot more and will try nagging a bit less, according to Mexico.
- Faced with limited success, Russia has recently hinted it may accept a more casual relationship, such as overlord with benefits.

The China analysts weren't about to take this quietly and produced their own analysis, mimicking the impenetrable circumlocution often seen in their region:

China: Hu Makes a Journey, Dusty, Rapacious

Chinese President Hu Jintao (none other than the President of China) quietly, pleasantly, almost running, goes to Chinese Wal-Mart to buy toilet paper (it is the good kind, two-ply, not too rough). And so the time had come, and Grandfather waked him, and it was time. We assess:

- And Grandfather preferred to use bamboo as it was in the old days, yet it was not the old days.
- Heretofore he had always had his wife do the shopping. But she (the wife) did not this time. He did. He felt ambivalent, but with a certainty, gesturing, thickfooted, he shuffled through the streets, bright and cold.
- Hu remembered Uncle Ming holding his hand, Ming (the elder) and Hu going to Wal-Mart together. Ming held his hand. He ought to have done it (gone to Wal-mart) last week. Mrs. Hu would be angry. She oughtn't be. She might have gone herself. But she didn't.

He enters into Wal-Mart gladly, the stockboys (there are many, smelling of fried scorpions) come running, surly, to help but that is why he is afraid. He knows them to be of an age which is twice the age of a normal stockboy, slouched, insolent.

- Disturbed but calm, he is both focused and confused. The toilet paper (gaunt, it is already soiled before it is used) is waiting for him, he reckons, but he goes to the snack foods aisle.
- He doesn't know what he wants. Uncle Ming once rode a giraffe to his own crucifixion, but it was too hot to bury him. So they put him in a landfill. He (Hu) had to escape but first he had to buy the toilet paper, *the Politburo will be angry.*

Hu paid the cashier (she was silent, vigilant, a guardian of the cashbox) as if she had never been paid before. Maybe she hadn't. He (the President of China) put two old renminbi in her hand, exactly what she asked for. *No that is not what she is asking for.* Then two old newspapers: they were rotten and smelled of apples.

He was walking along the road that would take him home, yet it seemed he was getting farther away yet than he had not planned to.

Grandfather was at the door. His pants (the old kind, from the days before the revolution) were deathcolored, and pungent. Hu vomited.

Very likely his wife (whether she was really his wife or not, he could not have said) was standing, impatient but virtuous. They talked, not talking: he stared at her face, which he had never seen before sweet lord Grandfather likes the toilet paper oh it stinks I'm too late.

Iraq-watchers got in the game with separate pieces:

To the Sadrists, To Make Much of Time (with apologies to Bob Dylan)

Turn in your AKs, while ye may,
    Old time is still a flyin',
And those JAM diehards who fight today,
    Tomorrow will be dying.
Our glorious leader, heaven's own son,

The holier he's a'getting.
The sooner he will end our fun,
   And his new rules be setting.
For war is that for which we thirst,
   When youth and blood are warmer,
But as we age, the worst and worst
   Times still succeed the former.
So be not coy, but use your time
   And of studies be not wary.
For if you still engage in crime,
   Tomorrow you we'll bury.

The Sadr Trilogy

Ed's note: In the first volume, we were treated to *The Hunt for Red October* as the Directorate of Intelligence would do it. That author's successors have examined what John LeCarre would face if he worked in the DI.

Tinker, Tailor, Student, Cleric…

The truth is, if old Major Dover hadn't dropped dead at Taunton races, Jim never would have come to CIA at all. He came in mid-term without an interview—in late May, it was, though no one would have thought it from the weather—employed through one of the shiftier agencies specializing in supplying contractors for DI Offices, to hold down old Dover's account until someone suitable could be found. "A linguist," Thursgood told the staff meeting, "a temporary measure," and brushed away his forelock in self-defense. "Priddo." He gave the spelling, "P-r-i-d"—French was not Thursgood's subject so he consulted a slip of paper—"e-a-u-x, first name James I think he'll do us very well till July." The staffer had no difficulty reading the signals. Jim Prideuax was a poor white of the analytical community. He belonged to the same sad bunch as the late Mrs. Loveday, who had a Persian-lamb coat and stood in for junior leadership until her cheques bounced, or the late Mr. Maltby, the targeteer who had been called from choir practice to help the police with their inquiries, and as far as anyone knew was helping them to this day, for Maltby's box still lay in the copier room awaiting instructions.

Jim Prideaux arrived on a Friday afternoon in a rainstorm. He worried that this kind of stuff might go on for many chapters, dulling his interest in what he anticipated would be a gripping plot that plumbed the depths of human motivation and explored the moral ambiguities of his profession. Fortunately, this was not the Circus, and George Smiley was unlikely to emerge from the rainstorm and summon him from his trailer to hunt down a mole. No, this was the DI, and that kind of writing would not be tolerated.

Although, since he worked in OIA, he was in a trailer...

The Honourable Schoolboy

Afterwards, in the dusty little corners where DI officers meet, there was an argument about where the Sadr Transformation case history really should begin. The debate continues, wherever old comrades should meet, though the name of Akram al-Kabi understandably is seldom mentioned. Only the other day, a young analyst just out of the Agency's refurbished CAP program in the jargon, again, the nursery—piped it out in the under 30s happy hour. (*Ed's note:* CAP: Career Analyst training.)

"But my God," he protested, enjoying the kind of fool's freedom sometimes granted to analysts in a brown bag with the DI, "my God, why does nobody seem to recognize al Kabi's part in the affair? Al Kabi carried the lead. He was the spearhead. Well, wasn't he really?"

Chief Targeting Team fielded the loose ball. C/TT is tall and tough and graceful, and analysts waiting a first TDY to Baghdad tend to look up to him as some sort of Greek god. "Al Kabi was the stick that poked the fire," he said curtly, ending the silence. "Any rogue Sadrist would have done as well, some a damn sight better."

When the boy still did not take the hint, C/TT rose and went over to him and, very pale, snapped into his ear that he should buy himself another drink if he could hold it and thereafter guard his tongue for several days or weeks. Surprisingly enough, the analyst shut up and did what he was told, even though he was a millennial.

Perhaps a more realistic point of departure is a certain rainy Saturday in mid-2008, three o'clock in the afternoon, when Qom lay battened down waiting for the next onslaught. In the bar of the Foreign Correspondents Club, a score of journalists and one young clerical student fooled and drank (tea, I swear!) in a mood of violent idleness. Sadr listened, rapt really, as the now ancient Australian Craw, still wearing his famous straw hat, unwound his tale of love and honor and the rebirth of British intelligence through perfidious manipulation of two brothers' love for each other. The story had everything. Intrigue and betrayal, opium dens in Phnom Penh, a lovely tart laundering money for Soviets and their Chinese Communist Christian asset who loved his brother more than Sadr had ever loved his brothers. And war. Lots and lots of war.

Sadr was utterly disgusted but not at all surprised. This was the way foreigners acted. And why he had to get them out of his country. Still, it did remind him that Akram al-Kabi was traitorously trying to take over his movement and that his father had always said war was bad. Perhaps he should change his ways.

Sadr's People

The leader saw a chance to strike one more blow for the cause. Exiled in Iran, studying to raise his rank, even if only in the eyes of his hosts, he knew it was critical to change direction or the movement would end up just one more sad collection of aging émigrés living out past glories. If that was the case, he might as well move to Paris.

The key, as always, was getting the message delivered. The phone wouldn't do; he needed the proof and a trusted courier to take it. Too bad his cousin's son was driving a lorry in England. He'd have to use al-Araji, Shaybani and others of his fieldmen to spread the message and hope that, for once, they didn't turn some side deal or get distracted by an attractive blonde.

The contents of the message were, of course, much less interesting than the tradecraft of moving it. No photos of Maliki in a compromising position or proof he'd been embezzling state funds to house his daughter in a Swiss asylum. The real world was much less interesting. The letter simply ordered his movement to stop fighting and instead turn to studies and charity. He'd keep a remnant of scalp hunters and stinks and bangs men, but they'd be definitely kept in mothballs.

A pity, really, to stand down his army of lamplighters and wranglers and street artists; those petty assassins and con artists, thieves, and smugglers. But Iraq had changed. And he had to change with it. Besides, he'd still have the burrowers. They could stay.

One can never have enough analysts.

THE DIA ANALYSIST: DIA'S MONTHLY UNDERGROUND PUBLICATION
Shouting Truth at Power Since 2009

DIA's humor comes out right on schedule, starting in mid-2009, when *The Analysist Quarterly*, motto *In Satura Verum*, Persistence in Lampooning the Agency, snuck into analysts' in-boxes. DIA humor doesn't end with the self-deprecating "Discount Intelligence Agency" version of its name. Herewith, a sampling of Analysist articles from the November 2009 edition:

// ⊕ //

DU Announces Yet Another Rotation: Let's Make a DEAL

In an attempt to meet the growing needs of Defense Intelligence Oficionados, the Director of Untelligence on Tuesday announced the creation of a new administration assistant rotation for highly qualified Band 4 employees. "We are pleased to announce the implementation of the Defense Enterprise Administration Liaisons," said DU spokesperson Linda Wallenstein. "The DEALs will alleviate the overwhelming demands of our DIOs, who just have so much to do," she added.

According to Wallenstein, the DIOs, burdened with coordinating intelligence across the Defense Intelligence Enterprise, have been lagging behind in other areas. The DEALs will assist them in accomplishing the more mundane, administrative tasks, such as turning in their time sheets and travel vouchers, paying their bills, and picking up their dry cleaning.

"I was a little unsure about the position at first," said Harold Finefeuiaki, formerly of the Mass Transit Systems Office, Entire-World-Except-for-Afghanistan Division. "I mean, it sounded a little demeaning, but when I got selected to assist the DIO for Cote-d'Ivoire, I realized that I either had to find a new job and learn a completely new skills set, or I could just bite the bullet and view this rotation as a chance to recharge my intellectual batteries."

Not everyone is satisfied with their new position, however. Matthew Lipke of the Proliferation of Over-the-Counter Medications Division finds his job as DEAL for Small-Arms/Light Weapons unrewarding. "Nobody asked me or thought about whether it would help my career," he said. "The worst part is my DIO is 26 years old. I own handguns older than her."

Lipke also said he was annoyed that he now had to submit all paperwork electronically. "I used to do all that hardcopy. Now it takes me two days to fill in a timesheet that used to only take me a couple of hours."

Wallenstein maintains that the DEAL rotation is temporary. "Only until the DIOs have a standard job description," she said.

// ⊕ //

Optimistic New Analyst Incites Laughter, Pity

For Aaron Bradford, the job offer from DIA is a dream come true.

"I never thought that a kid from North Dakota would step right out of college into such a dynamic position. This proves that with hard work anyone can do great things."

Recently graduated from Dakota Wesleyan University in Mitchell, SD, Aaron recalls some skepticism about leaving home to attend college in the city, but now believes it was the right choice.

"Although Rugby, ND is the county seat, a first job making $30,000 a year is unheard of, let alone the $42,000 I will be raking in. My mom almost fainted when I told her the news."

Bradford's pride, however, has sparked mixed reactions from future co-workers. Alex McGaylan recalls their first conversation, stating "I called Aaron to let him know that I was his sponsor, and he just said the craziest things."

According to MacGaylan, "Aaron said something about being ready to 'give his life for his nation.' At first I said 'Yeah, as the Botswana navy analyst you usually live life on the edge.' But when he answered, 'I hope I'm up for it,' my appendix nearly burst holding in the laughter!"

(At the jump page, the subtitle was *Clueless Analyst Has Much To Learn*)

Bradford's comments also sparked less jovial reactions.

"That poor kid," laments Janice Baker senior analyst and former Rhodes Scholar. "Will he be able to maintain a shred of hope or identity after 5 months of training? All of those classes? All the PowerPoint?" Staring into the distance, she added, "There is nothing worse than seeing bureaucracy crush your dreams."

While excited for his future, Bradford knows that he can't rest on his laurels.

"At first, I'll probably have to settle for a small place, maybe 5 acres or so. But with hard work and this new 'pay for performance,' in 10 years or so I could be making $60,000, even $70,000! That's more than anyone in Rugby."

Seeing a map of Washington, DC for the first time in his life, Bradford smiles and adds, "Oxon Hill, MD sounds like just the place for the son of a cattle farmer."

// ⊕ //

USA Today Making Move to Acquire DUD

The *Defense Untelligence Digest* may look different very soon. Media conglomerate Gannett Company, Inc., owner of *USA Today*, is looking to expand into intelligence production.

"We think the *DUD* would be a perfect addition to the Gannett family," said Craig Dubow, CEO of Gannett. He admitted that while the prospect of taking over DIA's flagship publication was rather intimidating, he believes that the *DUD* would complement Gannett's holdings. Dubow also said that, if acquired, the *DUD's* day-to-day operations would be run by the editorial staff at *USA Today.*

(At the jump page, the subtitle was *"DUD Soon May Hit Newsstands, Fast Food Restaurants"*)

USA Today, known for its colorful pages and *Reader's Digest* caliber news, refused to comment on the possible acquisition or any plans it may have to reengineer the publication for a wider audience. However, they did release an official statement: "We confirm our parent company, Gannett Co., Inc. has notified us they are considering placing us in charge of the *Defense Unintelligence Digest.* We wish to assure the Defense Intelligence Agency, the larger Intelligence Community, and all federal consumers of intelligence that we take very seriously the possible stewardship of such a prestigious publication. We will do our utmost to ensure the outstanding quality heretofore displayed be maintained in an unclassified environment."

Many at DIA are less than confident of *USA Today's* ability to branch out into intelligence. "I don't think it's a good idea," said Robert Lazenki, current *DUD* Editor-in-Chief. "Our strength is that we appeal to a wide range of policy-makers. Anyone from the most junior member of Congress to the members of the National Security Council can read a *DUD* article with no background on the subject matter, and they will glean enough knowledge to make important decisions regarding US national security. If this deal happens, we'll just become McIntelligence."

Dubow denied any degradation of quality would occur. "I strongly resent the accusation that we would run the *DUD.* That's as offensive as calling *USA Today* 'McNews.'"

// ⊕ //

The Tone Box

Q: How many CIA agents does it take to change a light bulb?

A: I'm sorry, that information is classified.

// ⊕ //

CFC Lottery Exceeds Double Eagle Expectations, the Law

You may have noticed the CFC lottery number in your inbox last week. If not, you're one of the lucky few. Dozens of people were called into the DIA's Coercive Federal Collection headquarters last week because their numbers were randomly drawn. "We needed a way to ensure that DIA remained at the cutting edge of charitable donations, as we were seeing signs of a donation gap," said CFC Chair Michelle Limburger.

Felix Cumpleanos, Band 2 analyst, was called in and shown pictured of homeless kittens and flooded rec centers until he agreed to donate 2 percent of his salary to the CFC general fund. "I originally intended to donate," he complained, "until I was told we weren't getting raises this year. They raised my rent—I was barely living paycheck to paycheck. Now I have to get a second job to pay for my donation."

"Look, we never forced anyone to do anything," responded Limburger. "We merely suggested that it was in everyone's best interests to ensure DIA's reputation vice that of other DOD agencies didn't suffer. Have you seen that campaign board at the Pentagon? We're lagging behind the Defense Logistics Agency!"

The CFC may have overstepped its bounds, however, and dauntributions may be returned. "Admittedly, the CFC was a little overzealous, but the real issue was that fauxnators were told they had to donate to the general fund, rather than being allowed to choose their own charity," said Frances Brubaker of the CFC Enforcement Division. "Given the economic crisis, it's not surprising that DIA did what it did to remain at the bleeding edge of caring."

DUPON

The bearer of this DU coupon is entitled to one hassle-free review session with their Senior Intelligence Officer. Upon redemption, said SIO shall limit the review session to no more than 15 minutes, shall resist inserting their own voice into the product, and shall refrain from physical violence.

DIA Requests Federal Bailout Over DCIPS

In an ironic twist of fate, DIA on Thursday became the first federal body to declare bankruptcy and request a bailout from Congress.

Captain of Personnel Wilford S. Tepperton, Jr., explained how the agency—known for its puppy-dog-seeking-approval eagerness in implementing any initiative sneezed out of the Office of the Director of National I'm-With-CIA—reached such dire financial circumstances.

"Basically, when we converted to DCIPS, we did so in a relatively short period of time. That meant that all pay raises would be scheduled during a narrow timeframe. Under the newly old pay-for-performance system, we figured we were safe. We expected a large portion of the workforce to receive 'Marginally Unsuccessful' appraisals, resulting in a negligible bump in salary." (*Ed's note:* DCIPS: Defense Civilian Intelligence Personnel System.)

Tepperton admitted that the Agency was not prepared for the decision to place pay-for-performance on hold and issue step-increase-like raises to all employees.

"We are completely at a loss. We used to spread out raises throughout the year, one pay period at a time. Now we have to frantically rush to get them all done at the beginning of the fiscal year, before we have the funds to do so. Frankly, we haven't got the budget to do that. I guess I shouldn't be surprised, though. We implement most of our programs that way, like the way to hectically start paying attention to employee complaints right before we roll out the WE Survey each year."

Congresswoman Eleanor Holmes Norton chastised the agency for its lack of foresight. "If I had a vote, I'd kick these clowns right out of my District. They're going under, and then I'll have yet another vacant lot to worry about."

Hope is not completely lost for the ailing intelligence agency, however. Rumors currently circulating in the Maryland *Pennysaver* indicate that Citigroup may consider investing some of its TARP money in order to acquire DIA's Forensic Financial Analysis Division. AQ predicts this trend may extend to other DIA offices. Coming soon: Energy Analysis brought to you by Jiffy Lube.

// ⊕ //

Did You Know?

Contrary to popular misconception, DIA employees do not begin their day when they log into their workstation. Rather, your work day begins when you swipe your badge at the front gate and ends when you swipe out. So go ahead, grab that cup of coffee, check the gift shop for good deals on DIA swag, and visit with all your friends as you head to your desk. You're already on the clock.

// ⊕ //

2009 WC Survey to Include Changes

It's that time of year again: time to let your voice be heard in the voting booth and in the halls of DIA through the annual Workforce Chattel Survey.

"The Survey is everyone's opportunity to let our management know what a wonderful job they are doing," said WC representative Stacey Howe. "This year, we're particularly excited, because we're slightly altering the survey to help simplify our review of the data."

In order to streamline the evaluation of the Survey results, WC has added the Myers-Briggs Type Indicator questionnaire to the standard questions about the Agency. "Last year, it took us dozens of minutes to tabulate the results, and months to put it all together in a spreadsheet. There were just so many complaints! Then there was the lengthy review process and getting senior executives to approve the results. It was a nightmare!"

However explained the reasoning behind their decision. "We originally planned to require respondents to indicate their age. That way, we could immediately identify and weed out the Gen Y-ers—I mean, their sense of entitlement is outrageous—but Generic Counsel told us that was illegal."

However, by having people identify their personality types, which are not protected by law, WC can easily identify those predisposed to incessant complaining. "We're especially looking out for the INTPs. Since we know that nothing DIA does will ever be good enough for them, knowing who they are allows us to discount their feedback from the start."

Howe said she does not question the ethics of this new approach to the Survey. "Everyone tries to put their best foot forward, right? But sometimes, some people here don't know how to do that. This way, WC can do it for them."

// ⊕ //

Pay Band 6s to File Class-Action Complaint

Pay Band 6 civilian employees will file a class-action complaint in a bold gambit to halt what they view as systemic promotion discrimination under the now semi-abandoned DCIPS pay-for-performance system. Under DCIPS, the majority of the agency's workforce is Pay Band 6 (nearly 80% by some estimates), with few promotion opportunities other than infrequent vacancy announcements.

Following news that Band 7 employees will be encouraged to call "first dibs on promotion opportunities," or FDOPO, to prevent the ascendancy of pay band 6s to positions of power, the stage was set for an inter-agency pay band revolt. "This is malarkey," says Frank Z. "I was passed over for a Band 7 position, all because I got FDOPO'ed. I found out they didn't even interview the incumbent—in fact, the incumbent wasn't even looking for a new job!"

The class-action complaint is now being filed with the Human Enterprise Resolution Solutions Directorate on behalf of all the agency's Band 6 personnel. However, no employees are seeking financial compensation from the complaint. "This is about equality," says the attorney for the 6s. "If it happens that a Pay Band 6 is the most qualified candidate for the job, they shouldn't be reduced to a number. They just want a chance to compete."

The class-action complaint seeks to add the following language to all agency internal communiqués: "The agency is an equal opportunity employer, and does not discriminate against any gender, race, creed, age, orientation, physical disability or pay band."

The Art of Intelligence
DID It
Music by Devo
Lyrics by BeeBee and the Malcontents

>   Write that *DID*
>   Give the boss a thrill
>   Craft that phrase
>   Make it fill the space
>   When a crisis comes along

You must *DID* it
When you boss's face is long
You must *DID* it
When you quota is just wrong
You must *DID* it
Now *DID* it
Work it hard
Write it short
Quick suspenses
Tradecraft
Pithy endnotes
Graphics, too
Collaborate it
FDO it
Release it, too
Metadata
DID it good

DIA Chief of the Office of Useless Projects announced her decision to endow the Falco Chair of Art and Intelligence at the National Defense Intelligence College on Tuesday. Chair Florence Henderson's first grand was to Devo cover band BeeBee and the Malcontents.

Falco Chair Florence Henderson is pleased to announce NDIC's first annual Intelligence Haiku Contest. "As a long-time fan of poetry, I think DIA owes it to the country to explore this powerful medium as a method of disseminating finished intelligence… Oh, look, I just used professional jargon!" said Henderson. Submissions may be sent directly to Dr. Henderson. She released this recently declassified haiku as an example of what she was looking for:

Missiles in Cuba
They look pretty Soviet
Recommend blockade

"I just think if imagery analysts had led with that rather than waiting for photos, we would have saved a lot of time and we could have avoided the crisis," said Henderson.

// ⊕ //

Source Summary Statement

All names, offices, situations, and gaffes in this publication are purely fictional. Any similarities with real persons or blunders may not be coincidental, but they are intended only to make good clean fun of human foibles and the absurdities of government bureaucracy. All persons offended by any material within this publication should attempt to apply the common sense test, or at least try some introspection, prior to complaining. –*Lucilius, Editor-in-Chief*

// ⊕ //

Performance

Face it—those at the top just aren't judged by the same criteria you are. Now dance, monkey, dance.

// ⊕ //

Awards, Announcements, and Administrivia

- Lost: locked courier pouch. Last seen in Pentagon cafeteria, near Starbucks. If found, please contact [redacted].
- Congratulations to Josie Swarnes for completing DIA's anger management course. Swarnes is the 83rd and final analyst from the Mongolia Regional division to complete the training. That division must be full of calm, serene employees!
- Beginning Thursday, the Contractors Teaching Military Intelligence Training Center will begin offering the *Combative Collaboration Course* to all employees. Learn how to evoke straight answers out of State INR, or get straight answers out of NSA. Discover effective methods of taking on overwhelming CIA numbers and breaking up their tag-team briefings. Come see how CTMITC can improve your hand-to-hand collaboration, professional relationships, and increase your emotional intelligence. Check NOZHR for details and course schedule.

- Reminder: Stricter password requirements for NIPRNET, SIPRNET, and JWICS will be enforced on Monday. Passwords need to be at least 25 non-repeating characters from the following categories: upper-case letters, lower-case letters, numbers, cuneiform, and punctuation marks. While two successive characters may be from the same category, the password cannot contain another pair from that same category, nor can a categorical pair occur for another five characters.

Ed's note: The January 2010 edition featured these gems:

Executive Order Reduces Wild Goose Chases by 87%

According to a joint study conducted by the US Government Accountability Office and the Department of Defense Inspector General's office, Executive Order 98554 has reduced wild goose chases within DoD intelligence agencies by 87%. Executive Order 98554, which prohibits officers O-6 and above from consuming open source media while on active duty, was enacted four months ago under recommendation of the Office of the Director of National Intelligence.

John Beauregard, Current Intelligence Division (Alert Watch Team 8), echoes the study's findings. "We've definitely noticed a difference here on the watch floor. Before, some O-6 would come in with their hair on fire and blabber about something they heard on NPR or news radio on their way into the office, and then we'd spend a majority of our shift jumping down rabbit holes. Now we can actually focus just on the message traffic coming in."

Maria De Soto, Joint Staff Presentations Branch (Current Operations Division), is equally pleased with the results of the EO. "Before, during slide briefings we would constantly be interrupted by Flag and General Officers who would say, "Well, I heard on BBC, or I read in Pakistani press this, or I saw on Fox News…" and we'd get totally side-tracked with non-issues. Now the discussion of the briefing slides is totally based on intelligence sources and open source reports that have been vetted by

OSC. If only they could legislate a way to keep Majors from thinking they're the smartest person in any room they walk into."

(Subtitle at jump page: *"EO Prohibits Officers from Acting Like Analysts"*)

The study also noted that the technical measures enacted to ensure compliance with Executive Order 98554 within the workplace have been implemented successfully. CNN has been replaced with a feed showing all the Army-Navy football games from 1978-2006 on a continuous loop, Fox News has been replaced with a feed showing gun camera footage, and Headline News has been replaced with a feed displaying police chases and animal attacks. DoD Computer System Operations Support has also installed the required O-6 unclass Internal portal which prohibits access to news sites, news blogs and news video feeds. Instead O-6 and above users are routed to DoD approved websites such as icanhascheezburger, funnyordie, hulu, ESPN, youtube, fantasy sports and game sites.

Analyst Censured for Failing to Coordinate Lunch Plans

Wendy Clawson of the Cameroon Air Forces Division was officially reprimanded last week for attempting to take her lunch break alone. "I'm reading the new Dan Brown book and just wanted to eat by myself and read," she said. Unfortunately, that idea resulted in an official letter of record further marring her already blemished record.

"That is just the sort of thing we've been trying to stamp out around here. She's well aware of our policy and chose to be insubordinate anyway," said Paula Whitmore, her supervisor. According to Whitmore, CAFD has implemented a strict Collaborative Lunch program, or CoLun, which requires division members to seek friendship and camaraderie with each other through shared meals. CoLun discourages individuals from shunning colleagues by seeking privacy. According to Whitmore, Clawson blatantly disregarded CoLun to finish a third-rate pulp novel.

"I just didn't think I could take another day of [name redacted] eating Hormel chili and belching at the table," Clawson said.

"That's no excuse," Whitmore said. "I've counseled her before about this sort of behavior. It's almost as bad as the time she blew off the division picnic to attend her sister's wedding."

// 🌐 //
SDUA Accidentally Reviews Own Product

Writing for the *Defense Untelligence Digest* is a rigorous exercise and is not for the faint of heart. However, at the end of the chop chain lies a polished, concise intelligence product that anyone can pick up and understand, regardless of whether they have any expertise in the topic or not. At least, that is the way the process usually works.

For Alan Baker, Stringent Defense Untelligence Approver for Vietnamese textile exports, the process backfired in a tragic chain of events.

"Ever since my promotion, I have had to wear two hats as both SDUA and analyst, as nobody was ever hired to replace me," said Baker. "So when the time came to write an article for the annual Alert issue, I was on the hook." He admitted, however, he was so attached to his old account that he didn't feel the other analysts in his office could write the product with the accuracy and nuance the topic deserved. "Nobody else understands the effect a cotton-poly blend has on the Vietnamese criminal underground," he said.

(Jump page subtitle: *"SDUA Blames Own Review Process for Mistake"*)

Baker wrote the required article on corruption in the Vietnamese leisure and business suit industry, and left it for his office SIO to review before he left for two weeks of leave. Unbeknownst to Baker, his SIO made liberal changes to the draft before turning it over to the *DUD* Staff.

Upon his return, Baker was asked to review the very product he had written. "I'd forgotten to put my name on it, so the *DUD* Staff had no idea I was the author. They just thought it was right up my alley," he said.

Baker dutifully reviewed the document and sent it back for the analyst to make the necessary changes. Only when his office SIO handed him his review of the draft did he realize what had happened. "Sally changed so much of the article that it looked nothing like what I'd originally written. Besides, I'd been away for two weeks and forgotten I'd written it in the first place."

Baker said the incident was an egregious conflict of interest, but when asked what measures could be taken to prevent future occurrences, he admitted he didn't know. "Normally, I like to sit down with the author, but as an SDUA reviewer, I have to keep my objectivity, which requires me to strictly protect my anonymity," he said.

// ⊕ //

Combined DCIPS/Composting Town Hall Goes Awry

Several members of the Directorate for Capitalizing on Humans (DCH) were injured from rotten food during yesterday's joint town hall on the Defense Civilian Punishment System (DCIPS) 'pause' combined with DIA's new compositing initiative by Mission Guidance and Education (MISGUIDED).

The meeting, advertised as "an opportunity to share your enthusiasm for DCIPS and environmentalism," began with MISGUIDED Hygiene and Sanitation Chief Bob Bunder's 137-slide brief on the superiority of the new composting program over previously-failed recycling programs. MISGUIDED representatives passed out examples of expired produce at the end, allowing attendees to experience the magic of composting firsthand.

"That mighta been our first mistake," said Bunder. "I never shoulda got folks so excited about composting. Talking about turning trash into dirt just gets me worked up, so I shoulda figured it would excite the whole crowd."

Following the composting brief, DCH representative Jane Booth presented an in-depth update of the current status of DCIPS. "I thought they were all cheering my name, 'Booooth!' when I gave them statistics on how many Band 3s would be Grade 11s vs. 12s during the pause," she said, picking watermelon rinds out of her hair. When she mentioned that DCH, in anticipation of Congress voting to keep DCIPS, had no plans for a reverse to the GG pay scale, the first projectile—a rotting head of lettuce—struck Booth. A general melee then ensued.

(Subtitle at jump page: *"MISGUIDED Attempts To Capitalize on DCIPS"*)

"I didn't throw that first one," said John Letus-Throgher. "I sat there as organized and composed as the DCIPS implementation." Upon realizing their salaries would be untouched, several Band 7s attempted to restore order only to be pelted themselves by decomposing produce. "In hindsight, we shoulda done the composting part last," said Bunder. "But you know, hindsight is 20/20. Hey, isn't that what DCH keeps saying about DCIPS?"

"We honestly believed there was a lot of synergy in co-promoting composting and DCIPS," said DCH Deputy Chief Layla Johnston. "Composting is about changing something nasty into something valuable, and that's what DCIPS is. We had no idea employees cared so much about salaries and bonuses! What hurts is that they didn't stop to consider our situation—we spent months designing the whole system only to have people not like it… I mean, we've got feelings, too!"

Bunder said the joint town hall was an attempt to improve attendance at MISGUIDED events, such as the Bathroom Claw Instructional Event last November. "We thought we had a chance to capitalize on the rousing success of DCIPS."

All joint town halls are suspended until further notice, such as New Cafeteria Taste Test/Mandatory AFPAK Rotations, and Rodent Poison Distribution/Language Testing and Proficiency Pay.

Quality Evaluation Board Blacklists Customer

DIA's Quality Evaluation Board never sleeps. The QEB works tirelessly to ensure that customers get top quality finished intelligence products regardless of cost or consequence. So the QEB gets a little peeved when said customers disregard all their hard work.

Daniel Kittermann, DASD for Antarctica Issues, committed a particularly heinous crime by liking a *DUD* article the QEB had previously determined was substandard. "Pearls before swine," said Tracy Simmons, Senior QEB evaluator. "We go to great lengths to ensure analysts are providing our customers the best possible product, and this idiot completely ignores our opinions. It's like offering someone a nice Adelegger but they say, 'No thanks, I'm just fine with this case of EZ Cheese,'" Simmons complained.

Kittermann was unavailable for comment, though his administrative assistant told AQ, "Normally, Dr. Kittermann finds the *DUD* to be riddled with stilted, awkward language that adheres to a very unsatisfying rigid formula. But the article on Argentinean fishing instability was a breath of fresh air. He found it very useful in preparing for his trip to Caracas."

(Jump page subtitle: *"QEB Berates DASD for Low Standards"*)

"That piece of tripe? It only used twenty-three sources, and the key assessment said 'judges' when almost all the sources might possibly have been denial and deception attempts, which clearly mean low confidence," Simmons responded. "Besides, the article kept confusing me with Argentine and Antarctic fishing waters. Antarctica is a whole continent away from there!"

Consequently, the QEB is petitioning OSD to revoke Kittermann's security clearance, thus denying him access to all future intelligence products. "It's a matter of propriety," said Simmons. "Do we really want someone like that having access to intelligence?"

"I don't think they have a snowball's chance," said Kittermann's assistant, "with the surge coming up, DoD will need an experienced hand dealing with Antarctic issues."

// ⊕ //

Bright-Eyed College Students Eager to Work at DIA

Former DIA employee and current college career counselor Geraldine Thudpucker reports a steady stream of college students coming into her office, eager to learn how to obtain a career at the nation's premier intelligence agency.

"Of course," says Thudpucker, "they are disappointed when they learn I only have information on DIA and not CIA." Thudpucker does not take offense at the confusion. "It's only natural since no one has ever heard of DIA," she says.

Nonetheless, some students are genuinely interested in applying to DIA, believing it will be easier to get a job there than at more prestigious agencies. Thudpucker has encouraging words for these students: "That's exactly how I started working at DIA myself!"

Many students see a career at DIA as an exciting opportunity to use their skills in a stimulating atmosphere to address the nation's most critical security concerns. Thudpucker finds advising these students to be a particularly rewarding experience. "These students are just like I was ten years ago," says Thudpucker. "If only someone had been there to disabuse me of these notions then, like I am doing for these students now."

Thudpucker is happy to answer any questions students might have about working at DIA. She often describes her own career progression from writing critical time-sensitive intelligence products on an almost daily basis to becoming a member of a ten-person production chain which collectively produced about one product per week on events two months old. She is also accustomed to watching her students' expressions change from interest to confusion to horror when she is asked to describe DIA's organizational structure. However, Thudpucker's favorite student question was about morale at DIA. "I couldn't stop laughing for 5 minutes," she reports.

(Subtitle at jump page: "*Students Get Answers, Life Lessons About DIA*")

Several students have approached Thudpucker to ask how the Intelligence Community got its intelligence on Iraqi WMD so horribly wrong. Thudpucker explains that the IC at that time suffered from critical shortages in critical thinking training, number of reviewers, confidence language charts, source summary statements, and, of course, graphics.

Students often wonder how hard it is to get a job at DIA. Thudpucker explains that she herself benefited from the post-September 11 hiring boom: "The September 11 attacks dramatically increased the need for Chilean military agriculture analysts such as myself." Hiring is a bit tighter today, but Thudpucker encourages her students not to lose hope: "I assess with moderate-to-high confidence that I cannot rule out the possibility that at least one of them may get a job."

// ⊕ //

Did You Know?

Workforce Chattel estimates that about 42 percent of all DIA employees are undiagnosed "psychophants." That is, they are so eager to further their careers that they have no moral qualms about committing violent acts in the process of sucking up, brown-nosing, backstabbing, or otherwise stepping on the necks of their co-workers. SO you have an almost even chance of either being a psychophant yourself or sitting next to one.

// ⊕ //

DUPON

The bearer of this DU coupon is entitled to a pass on the next Analytic Quality Day, regardless of whether the bearer is an attendee or a presenter. The dupon must be presented to your immediate supervisor upon request and works best when accompanied by a doctor's note, back brace, full-body cast, iron lung, evidence of severe head trauma or thoracic surgery, or a death certificate.

// ⊕ //

The Tone Box

One of the FBI's best marksmen was passing through a small town. Everywhere he looked—on trees, walls, barn doors, and fences—he saw bull's-eyes with the bullet hole dead center. The agent man asked one of the townsmen if he could meet the person responsible for this amazing marksmanship. The man turned out to be the village idiot.

"This is the best marksmanship I have ever seen," said the FBI man. "How in the world do you do it?"

"Nothing to it," said Cletus. "I shoot first and the draw the circles afterward."

// ⊕ //

The Art of Intelligence

The Tradecraft is A-Changing'
Music by Bob Dylan, Lyrics by anon.

    Come gather 'round analysts
    Wherever you write
    And remember you are
    This agency's blight
    And without my direction
    You won't last through the night
    If your job to you
    Is worth savin'
    Then you better start thinkin'
    And be critically right
    For the tradecraft is a–changin'.
    Come SIAs, SIOs

Who criticize with your pen
Don't think we can't live
Without all your comments
And don't change our words
To what you think they meant
Then have the gall to
Call it editin'
They who's Band 4 now
Will be Band 3 again
For the tradecraft is a-changin'.
Come CIA, DIA
Please heed the call
Tear down all your stovepipes
Don't build up your walls
For he who builds highest
Has furthest to fall
The collaboration
Is outragin'
It'll shift all paradigms
And force you to call
Out that tradecraft is a-changin'.
Come senior executives
Who dispense from your hand
Many policies
That we just don't understand
But despite our confusion
You doggedly command
Your old management
Style is agin'
So decide whether or not
We're going to payband
For the tradecraft is a-changin'.
The conclusion is drawn
The BLUF it's up front
The assessment

Is perfectly blunt
But all your hard work
Aside they will shunt
Your status is
Rapidly fadin'
As in-depth reports
They readily punt
For the tradecraft is a-changin'.

// ⊕ //

Supervisors

They're like tires. Some are spares, but most are flats.

// ⊕ //

Awards, Announcements, and Administrivia

- As we begin the new year, we at AQ wish to thank all those who so consistently provide us with dynamic material for this publication. There are too many to thank individually, and if you were at all self-aware, we'd probably have a lot less inspiration. Even though you have no idea who you are, we thank you anyway!
- Milton Addams of the North African Refrigeration Technologies Division offers a reward for any information leading to the return of his red Swingline stapler. The ratio of people to staplers is too large, and we wouldn't want him to burn this place to the ground.
- Congratulations to Willa Patterson for publishing her 300th article on Nauruan political-military issues. We're proud of your crucial contributions to the pursuit of excellence in service of the national defense!
- Facilities Usage (FACU) personnel invite those with experience in painting unconventional surfaces to train personnel on how to paint parking lines in the gravel lot. While overtime is not authorized, the first five volunteers will receive a $3.50 gift certificate to the cafeteria.
- FACU would also like to reiterate that placing information, such as birthday announcements, retirement celebrations,

or the location of the nearest fire exits of lactation rooms, in any of the restrooms at the DIAC is strictly prohibited. Such trivial matters may be posted on the bulletin board hung by the service entrance, which has been reserved for your convenience.

A VISIT TO NSA

The National Security Agency is arguably the most secret institution within the US Intelligence Community. Its denizens also tend toward being guarded, with introversion a standard personality trait. The standard joke is "How can you tell the extravert at NSA?" "He looks at your shoes when he's talking to you."

The Snowden revelations in 2013 of NSA collection on telephone and Internet activities led to the following suggestions for organizational mottos:
- NSA: We're the only part of government that listens to you!
- NSA: We're peeping while you're sleeping!

Following Russian language training, I spent three years at NSA. The first year was filled with constant security briefings about no foreign contacts, almost to the point that you are afraid to go to a Chinese restaurant. I had rented a home from a German doctor who was a fellow bird watcher. Later I shared part of the house with a young new NSA employee who worked the night shift. When I came home one afternoon, he told me, "You got a phone call from a foreigner. You are not supposed to have contact with foreigners. She said, Tell Lt. Levine 'dat die black svans are flying' and hung up. I have to report this to Security." Later on, NSA obtained a computer that was so fast that there was no name for the speed, which was above the current generation, the yottaflop, 1024 operations per second. One of the unbreakable codes they continue to work on in the background is "die black svans are flying".

// 🌐 //

Thanks to the NSA's *Cryptologic Quarterly*, Center for Cryptologic History, and Chief of Operational History at NSA, David H. Hatch put together a guide to the often mysterious dialect of English spoken at NSA. Hatch recalls, "recently, when seeing the definition for a traffic analytic term in a well-documented Agency working aid, it occurred to me that NSA is rich in unofficial vocabulary that has yet to make it into any sanctioned publication or official working aid. There is an extensive body of jargon used not only to make the cryptologic business seem arcane and exalted to outsiders but also to describe the many nonprofessional and unprofessional aspects of life at the Agency."

Architect: to structure units to perform a specific function or series of functions. For example, NSA must architect offices to provide support to the US Central Command. The panoply of organizations thus arrayed may be called the "architecture" for that particular purpose, as in the "crisis response architecture".

Badger: a worker's clearance status as marked for easy recognition by the color of his or her badge: green, red, or black—for fully cleared, noncleared, or contractor, respectively. (*Ed's note*: this color palette is not standardized throughout the rest of the Intelligence Community.)

Burn: to reproduce xerographically; a burn machine was an early office reproduction machine.

Burn bag: a heavy paper bag, resembling a grocery bag but without pictures of lost Agency employees on the side, used to collect paper trash for eventual destruction; the term has persisted long after fire was abandoned as a method of disposing of this waste.

Cans: earphones, especially when used during monitoring duty.

Cardiac Hill: the near-perpendicular parking area adjacent to the FANX complex; not for couch potatoes.

Checker's Choice: the ultimate recourse on questions arising in translation or transcription of foreign language material, in which the "checker", a senior linguist, makes a decision between two uncertain alternatives; the invocation from which there is no appeal.

Chop: to initial for approval or as evidence that coordination among offices has been carried out; may be used as a noun or verb.

Consumer (aka Customer): those who receive NSA reports through regular distribution channels. This is an attempt to introduce terminology from business and commerce into the Intelligence Community.

C-Ref: short appellation for the Office of Central Reference (sometimes Central Research). The nickname has continued long after the organization was absorbed into another group and its official name changed.

Cryppie: a shortened former of "cryptanalyst" used (and taken) by some as affectionate, by others as derogatory—listen carefully for the tone of voice and check to see if the speaker is smiling.

Day Lady: a mildly pejorative term used by workers on evening or overnight shifts to describe a person of either sex who works only "normal business hours"; often characterized by a compulsive concern for wearing a necktie or avoiding jeans.

Desk Rats: that's OK, you know who you are.

Diddy Bopping: copying manual Morse transmissions.

Dip: short for "diplomatic", denoting a type of traffic.

Fanfold: a method of printing multiple copies of a text; so called because the method used several-ply paper of different colors that resembled a lady's fan when spread out.

Flag Carriers: Agency senior executives, so named because the backdrop for their badge photographs includes an American flag.

Fort Fumble: a not altogether affectionate designation for Fort Meade and the NSA headquarters for those stationed elsewhere.

Friedman: shorthand designation for the largest auditorium in the Sigint City (q.v.); believed to be the only portion of the City actually named after an individual, in this case William F. Friedman (1891-1969), the dean of modern American cryptologists.

Ghost: to float among offices while awaiting a permanent position. (*Ed's note:* The CIA equivalent is "hall walker".)

Golf Ball: the spherical shield placed over antennas or other equipment to protect them from weathering or surveillance. When four of these were lined up atop the headquarters building in the 1970s, it was common to hear them described as "on, volume, horizontal, and vertical" knobs.

Gravel Pit: an unpaved parking area outside Gate 2, which featured either sandstorms or mudholes in season and not much in between. It was paved in 1989.

Hall, the: short for Arlington Hall in Virginia, once one of the main locations for the NSA, in latter years the headquarters of the Army Security Agency (now Intelligence and Security Command). This was a former private girl's school purchased by the military during WWII. See also Nebraska Avenue on next page.

Hammered: describes text with a significant number of garbles, misprints, or omissions that render it unreadable or call into question its validity.

Holy Joe, aka shotgun envelope: an interoffice distribution envelope with regularly spaced circular holes. The name is a play on the now obsolete nickname for an aggressive religious proselytizer.

Hours of Boredom/Moments of Terror: an unofficial slogan used to describe duty in NSOC or other watch offices.

Knobbing: the act of searching for target communications by twisting a dial manually on intercept equipment.

Korling: acronym for "Korean linguist", an occupation specialty. It would look less like a Scottish sport of Canadian beer if spelled with a hyphen.

Lingie: an attempt to create a nickname derived from the occupational specialty "linguist". Fortunately, this did not come into common use. Some linguists would prefer the phrase "language engineer" to describe their profession.

Mom's: a nickname for the cafeteria, possibly derisive.

Nebraska Avenue: Washington, DC location that served as headquarters for the Naval Security Group and also at one time as one of the main locations for NSA prior to its move to Fort Meade. Also see The Hall.

Ninth Floor: The location of the Director's office during most of the 1960s, 1970s, and 1980s, thus a synonym for the Agency's senior leadership or the final policy decision.

Other Side of the House: a relative term, dependent on the wing in which the speaker is located, referring to the dual function of signals intelligence and information security; each is the "other side" to its counterpart—for example, the "SIGINT side of the house". Many, however, regard the cryptologic community as polygonal, and refer to various necessary functions with this term, as in the "communications side of the house". (*Ed's* *note:* The same term is used in CIA to refer to the gulf between the analysts and the operatives.)

Problem: A particular target area, e.g., the Poinctesme Problem or, more specifically, the Coastaguena Naval Problem. See also Shop.

Retread: to retain an individual from a different occupational specialty; not to be confused with cross-training, which implied preparation for a position requiring knowledge of two specialties.

School, The: National Cryptologic School or its predecessor organizations; used even during periods when "the School" did exist as a discrete organizational entity.

Shop: the location—physical or figurative—for analysis of a particular target, as in the "Ruritanian shop"; sometimes also more specific, as in the "Erewhon air force shop". This is another example of the transference of vocabulary from business and industry to the cryptologic organization. See also Problem.

Sigint City: a term that came into some currency at the end of the 1980s to refer to the complex of NSA buildings at Fort Meade, a reflection of the number of facilities and the wide area over which they were spread. While catchy in itself, the term inappropriately slights other important aspects of the NSA mission, for example, information security.

Slip and Slide: to idle or waste time.

Spaces: shorthand references to "cleared" or "secure spaces", i.e., the place where classified endeavors may be carried out.

Straphangers: people assigned or involved in a meeting or activity in excess of actual need, and often without responsibility; personnel auditing a meeting but not contributing; those "along for the ride" in any activity.

Walk the Halls: To be without a permanent assignment and in search of one after return from a field or long-term training assignment.

Whiffle: to read rapidly through a stack of traffic to cull out useable items; this term is becoming obsolete as computerization reduces the amount of printed traffic routinely delivered to analysts.

// ⊕ //

In the mid-1960s, the Navy section of NSA was in a 100-foot stretch of connected open bays. When young women walked by, the Navy officers rang a ship's bell of up to 8 rings, depending upon her judged beauty. This tradition ended when a woman complained to a Department Head that she had received only 6 rings.

// ⊕ //

NSA puts out a daily newsletter to its staff, which includes a "History Today" section. The April 1, 2005 edition included a reprint of *The Most Accurate Sigint Report I Ever Read:*

(U) At least two Soviet long range aviation TU-95 (Bear) heavy bombers (a blue dot and a red dot) flew off the edge of my map between 0030 and 0245Z on the 19th. (*Ed's Note:* (U): Unclassified.)

(U) The little blue dot started about four inches left of Dolon' Airfield at 0030Z and kept going to the right with the little red dot about two inches behind it all the way. They were in the vicinity of the "Y" in Stanovoy Khrebet at 0138Z and right in the middle of the second "O" in Sea of Okhotsk at 0205Z. They kept on going right on down to the middle of the big blue part of the map at 0234Z. The next pair of dots was on the wall next to the navy map (0245Z). Speeds of 26 to 35 inches per hour (IPH) were computed.

(U) Two similar dots (one purple and one brown) flew off the edge of my map back in March. They never returned and these probably won't. This will be a final report unless they show up on the Navy map.

The newsletter notes that this message was transmitted only by e-mail; nobody knows where it started. One can guess that a creative analyst on a very slow mid watch was the author. Made to look like an actual SIGINT report, with a Date-Time-Group of 191517Z NOV 77, a serial number, and all the right TAGS and DDIs, it really looked authentic.

However, there was a message with the same serial number released in 1977, and the only place this message appeared was on internal NSA e-mail exchanges. It's a shining example of humor in the workplace and the vivid imagination of an unknown NSAer.

// ⊕ //

And for NSArs who are to retire soon, colleagues offered ways to re-capture the magic of Fort Meade (NSA Headquarters) by reconfiguring one's home and family:

- Partition your living room into cubicles.
- Find the first available parking spot 1.3 miles from your house and walk in from there.
- Raise pigeons with bowel disorders in your garage ceiling area.
- Put on a blue blazer and greet everyone as they enter your house.
- Invite tons of uninterested neighbors over for a demo of your latest home project visions; make sure the demo is rigged to outperform real-life expectations.
- Delete all emails you receive that don't contain the phrase "Free Donuts" in the subject line.
- Buy a large capacity fully functional refrigerator for battery storage and make family members store their personal food in a small beat-up dormitory fridge. Only stock batteries in sizes that nobody needs.
- Hold family town meetings at home and put up blurry, difficult-to-interpret slides.

- Randomly decide to reorganize the kitchen to streamline its effectiveness. Label each shelf with a long string of meaningless alphanumeric characters and then insist that everyone refer to the shelves by their plain names.
- Complain every 6 months about space in the house and make everyone switch bedrooms.
- Put speed bumps and concrete jersey barriers in your driveway.
- Have your spouse submit a budget plan in April for the Fiscal Year that begins in October; release the funds next February. Complain that the family members' burn rate is too slow and they risk losing those funds.
- Call 10 different pizza delivery restaurants to ensure a competitive bid process. Then have the pizza rush delivered to a warehouse across town where it can sit for 3 days before someone calls you and tells you it has arrived.
- Conduct random exit inspections at your front door.
- Stock your refrigerator with diet, caffeine-free soda; also keep it completely empty during hot summer months.
- Completely disable your spouse's computer and insist you can't fix it until they send you an e-mail outlining the problem. Wait a few weeks since you only provide "bronze" service.
- Wait for the hottest, coldest, or wettest day of the year and conduct a home fire evacuation drill…or have a picnic.
- Put a little paper tent on the desk in your den that says "Area Secure".
- Cite your kids for leaving out floppy disks that aren't in the original shrink wrap.
- Ask the Post Office to stockpile your mail for at least two weeks and then cram it all into your mailbox one day.
- Stand in the middle of your cul-de-sac behind a pile of sandbags with a high-caliber assault rifle and sunglasses and check IDs.

- Authorize the kids a 2.7% raise in their allowance and then increase room and board by 3%.
- Put 20 paper tents all over your dining room table to advertise an upcoming event that nobody really cares about.
- Put an old fish sandwich in the fridge and go on vacation for a week.
- Locate the most comfortable area of your house, with a beautiful outside view, with perfect summer and winter climate control, and put storage shelves there.
- Hire a cleaning service to temporarily close your bathroom every day at the peak hours just before and after lunch.
- Put a sign on the curb in front of the house that says "30 minute work-related van pool executive visitor parking only until 1300".
- Rewire your house circuits to trip breakers anytime the microwave and coffee maker are simultaneously operating.
- Clean your coffee pot as often as you clean your gutters.
- Whenever you need to go out of the house for a while, sign out electronically on your computer, write a note on at least two different dry-erase boards, attach a yellow sticky to your computer, and have a nameplate that you can slide over along with a tiny magnet. Never provide more info than "Out" or "In Class" so that people will still have no clue of your whereabouts.
- Carry a cell phone at all times but don't give anyone the number.
- Whenever a family member's birthday is coming up, buy a card and sit it on the counter for a few weeks with a gift contribution envelope.
- Put a vending machine in the house at the end of the hallway. Stock it every 6 months and raise prices every 3 months.
- When you drive to Ocean City for vacation, stop for a meal at a cheap roadside stand and explain to the family that they're only authorized ¾ of per diem for a travel day.

- Find the worst picture of each family member and require them to wear it on a chain around their neck at all times while in your house.
- Ignore the overflowing soda can recycling bin and continue to delicately balance more and more cans on top until someone else finally gives up and empties it.
- Designate, in writing, your oldest child as acting head of the house if you'll be away for a few days.
- Always refer to your spouse as "acting deputy".
- Request that the county shut down all convenient parking areas in the neighborhood if there's a slight dusting of snow.
- Convert your closet to something that looks like an elevator, stand in there for 5 minutes with some total strangers, then go down the hall and take the steps.
- Put up posters around the house with common sense messages such as "Don't Talk to the Neighbors if They Don't Have a Need to Know", "Practice Good Security by Locking the Screen Door", or "Only You Can Put the Seat Down".
- Drive to the Harbor Tunnel toll booth, dim your lights, and show the attendant two forms of identification.
- Serve all family meals with undersized Styrofoam plates and cheap plastic utensils; justify this by putting up a sign that says "Steam Outage".
- After your child spends all day washing the car, cutting grass, doing laundry, and weeding the garden, give him an average performance appraisal since his stated objectives were to just make his bed.
- Don't buy any furniture that wasn't made by prisoners in Leavenworth, Kansas.
- When the phone rings pick it up and state the last 4 digits of your phone number.
- Figure out how to stock the house with pens and notepads now that you can't pilfer the stock room or vendor exhibits.
- When you have your next child, give it a name, but only refer to it as "that new guy".

- Modify your front door with a cipher lock. Ignore all buzzes from visitors; somebody else will surely get it eventually.
- Place all of the snack items from the pantry onto your countertop with prices marked on each box and a collection can nearby.
- Make your daughter's potential boyfriends fill out lengthy forms and advise them of your right to require background investigations and polygraphs.
- Designate your garage workshop as a secure facility and require two-person integrity when someone goes near your toolbox.
- Put classification markings and special handling caveats on the cookie recipes that were passed down to you from your grandmother.
- Mount a bunch of huge "golf ball" radomes on your roof over the TV antenna and satellite dish.
- Raise your garden by first putting 15 cubic yards of concrete around it to form a planter.
- When a repairman comes to the house, put on a badge with an "E", give him a red badge, then sit nearby on a chair and do a crossword puzzle.
- Place red strobe lights around the house and turn them on whenever you have visitors.
- Throw a black cloth over the bird house you're building on your workbench.
- Pass love notes to your spouse in envelopes that have "Your Eyes Only" and "Sensitive but Unclassified" stamped on the top and bottom, centered, both sides.
- Instead of doing yard work, lay on your hammock with a cold drink and tell your wife that you're just striving for a better work/life balance.
- Send everyone in the family annoying messages to let them know that you are going to re-boot the main house computer tomorrow morning at 4 a.m.

- Place barcodes on everything in the house and perform wall-to-wall inventory every 3 months.
- Poke holes in the roof to create leaks and then put tarps, funnels, and large trash cans everywhere.
- Tell your kids that you appreciate all of their work and that their efforts are critical to the future of the family. Then zero out the family budget line item for their allowance. Then tell them to continue doing chores for you and find someone else to fund it.
- Show your family how much you appreciate them by having morale-boosting picnics or theme park visits sometime in late October when the weather has turned frosty.
- Buy a real nice flat screen TV, suspend it from the ceiling in a corner of the room, and only show CNN on it.
- Replace your oak entertainment center with a row of solid steel 19" racks.
- Put all paper trash into paper grocery bags. Once a day, drop the bags down the laundry chute. If you don't have a laundry chute, designate a child to be responsible to take the sacks to the garage. However, the child can only take them to the garage within two 20-minute windows each week. If he misses a window, he has to store the sacks in his dresser until the next window comes up.
- Put a tool bag in the hallway. Set a highway construction blinker light in the middle of the hallway next to the bag.
- Remove the dining room table. Post a notice that this household is not authorized to have a conference area.
- When you receive an e-mail addressed to a large group of people, forward it to the same group of people but post "FYI" at the beginning.
- Turn every family activity into a meaningless acronym.
- Paint the hallways and exposed wall surfaces using paints acquired through the low bid process and in colors appearing on no known color chart; avoid any effort to achieve anything even remotely describable as aesthetically pleasing.

- Have the children stand in the foyer and sell boxes of a half dozen doughnuts at a dollar a doughnut; then ignore them and walk on by.
- Make all visitors and family members leave their personal electronics (cell phones, iPods, Blackberries) outside in the mailbox.
- Assign designated "stops" in the neighborhood to pick up and drop off your family members. Only drive around it on a one-directional, circular route.
- Encourage your family members to collaborate to accomplish household chores, but don't offer to increase their allowance if this causes them to do a better job.
- Block YouTube, Facebook, and blogs.
- Make your kids and spouse fill out timesheets and leave slips.
- Hang a flat panel display in the foyer with announcements to upcoming family events.
- Make spouse sign involuntary deployment agreement….involuntarily deploy spouse
- UII bar codes on all property (TV, electronic can opener, etc.)
- If friends bring electronics over they have to be checked in—only after their credentials are passed.
- Make your kids put in a ticket when they want to have a sleep over
- Adjust kids' allowance via a PeopleSoft app.
- Keep Netscape 4.7 on the desktop for all family users
- Tell your spouse they left her lights on by posting that to your blog.
- If your spouse asks for travel money, tell him to keep receipts and fax them to the B&F guys.
- Make your spouse provide you with some objectives.
- Every October put heavy pressure on your kids to donate 10% of their allowance to CFC. (*Ed's note:* Combined Federal Campaign charity clearinghouse.)

- Charge 10 cents if anyone needs a spoon or fork with dinner.
- Brick up all windows except for the spare bedroom where Grandma stays when she visits, because she's a "Senior".
- Reserve the closest parking space in the driveway for Grandma, even if she's only in the building ten days out of the year.
- Roll the operating system on your computer back at least two versions. Make sure all applications (word processor, spreadsheet, web browser) are at least 5 years out of date.
- Require your children to provide you weekly updates about how they are spending their allowance. Make them use an Excel spreadsheet in which they have to put the same information into multiple locations. Deduct from their allowance if the different entries don't match.
- Encourage communication and collaboration by moving each family member to a separate house. Make sure that the houses are in different neighborhoods.

AS IF THE DIRECTOR DOESN'T HAVE ENOUGH TO WORRY ABOUT

Far from being distant creatures known only by their official photos but never actually seen by the great unwashed, the IC agency leaders of today want to portray themselves as having the common touch. Gardens of social media fora have sprung up to give the average employee a chance to talk directly to the Director, or at least their assistants. Although the IC directors have billion-dollar decisions to make, oftentimes employees would have them divert their attention to less weighty matters. Many believe that the way to really get IC employees stirred up is to fiddle with their parking.

Herewith, a few examples of some of the issues that the Directors of the National Geospatial Intelligence Agency and the Defense Intelligence Agency have been asked to address:

// ⊕ //

As someone who has received a multitude of the dreaded automatic rejection e-mails from EZHR (DIA's easy-hire vacancy notice system)—The latest just came. Alas, dreams of a joyous three years in Berlin will not happen—may I humbly recommend that we adopt something perhaps more humane? The tone of the e-mail is such that EZHR might as well tack on additional insults—perhaps "and you look strange and smell bad, too." Granted, DIA nurtures their employees about as well as the proverbial animal that eats its own young. Still, surely there's someone out there who can think of a gentler way to deliver the bad news to job applicants.

// 🌐 //

Bring Your Child to Work Day appeared to be a great success. Congratulations to all involved. It raised an issue, though, that I hope to get clarified. I had always assumed that a "carpool" was 2 or more badged NGA employees in a single POV (Personally Owned Vehicle) or vanpool—the goal being to maximize parking availability and minimize the use of resources in traveling to/from NCE (NGA's Washington headquarters-East). Last Thursday I noticed a number of cars in the carpool parking with only one NGA employee and one or more children.

Moving forward I was hoping to clarify how the agency is defining a carpool. I'm certainly not begrudging the parents, just using it as an example, but bringing kids in your car is not the same as a carpool with other employees and does nothing to alleviate the parking crunch here. Would it be possible to clarify the intent and execution of NGA's definition of a carpool? Do you require more than 1 badged individual or do any extra persons in the car count towards the requirement for a carpool parking pass? Thank you!

// 🌐 //

Recently, employees who use e-cigarettes were directed to use them in the designated smoking sections of the campus. Isn't that akin to telling a former alcoholic to drink non-alcoholic beer but only inside a bar? That policy seems to undo all of the effort to people who are trying to quit smoking. Isn't there a more supportive and humane option we can offer in this situation?

// 🌐 //

I understand the need to ensure the safety of all personnel while on NGA property. What guidelines were used to limit a knife's blade length to 2.5" or less? I would like to be able to carry a Gerber/Leatherman multi-tool but I can't find one without a 3" blade. Is a 3" blade considered "lethal" whereas a 2.5" blade is considered "non-lethal"?

// 🌐 //

I know this is usually a forum for complaining about DIA services, but I just wanted to take a second to share some praise for an exemplary cafeteria employee! In these times of budget constraint, we all have to do our part to eliminate waste. To that end, I want to highlight the efforts of one of the fry cooks at the burger/grill section of the cafeteria! While removing chicken wings from the fryer, this outstanding public servant's partner dropped a large wing to the floor. While many of us (perhaps even most) would have thrown that wing (and the funds spent on it) away without a thought, this conscientious individual retrieved this errant wing and returned it to the warming oven to await consumption.

In our throw-away culture, this is the sort of economically and ecologically responsible behavior we should all seek to emulate in our daily lives. I hope my children can grow up in a world where our resources are used with such little waste.

Does anyone know if DIA (or greater DoD) has an anti-waste award, or perhaps a "Green" Award to recognize such contributions? And, if so, how would I go about nominating this everyday hero? Kudos, sir!

// ⊕ //

The gym here in St. Louis has a floor-to-ceiling fixed glass panel next to the glass door. The maintenance crew does a fantastic job of keeping that panel clean, to the extent that at night, if you don't pay attention, it looks as though it is an open entryway. This poses a problem for idiots like me. I've twice gone to the gym and, lost in my thoughts as I was walking up, bounced my face off the glass. It is somewhat painful. Upon mentioning this to be my team, I discovered that there are two other idiots in my office, although to their credit neither has ricocheted off the glass TWICE! I am in the TDOC, so I frequently work night shift and will possibly end up going to the gym in the dark again. I like my face, and my girlfriend does, too. Please help us protect it by asking the facilities crew to put up a poster or something on that land mine of a glass panel. Thanks!

// ⊕ //

Beautiful facility, however, my seat is right above the gym. Whenever there is a spin class or step aerobics, my desk shakes constantly. Additionally, whenever weight lifters drop weights, it feels and sounds like the building is collapsing. (You would have to be here to feel it.) I think the gym floors need more padding or something.

// ⊕ //

We have recognized the rights of the Gays and Lesbians, non-gender as a statement of diversity. Some of the women are dressing like men, wearing ties and shirts with very short hair cuts. On several occasions I have gone into the women's restroom and thought a man was using it. It is very disturbing. Others have also expressed this concern. Since we have unisex bathrooms on each floor in Building 36 (designed to accommodate these choices), would it be possible to have those who choose to look like a man use those restrooms?

// ⊕ //

I considered it unprofessional and insulting for X, an office director, to have inscribed his office name plate with "Supreme Leader".

// ⊕ //

I have heard that the NGA CIO (Chief Information Officer) has a speech writer. Is this true? Why does anyone at NGA need a speechwriter? How many speeches do the senior people or any NGA employee give that a speechwriter would be necessary? It seems to me this could be eliminated and that money could be spent on something more useful, like larger toilet paper holders in the bathrooms at NCE.

(*Compiler's note:* Speaking of toilet paper, when CIA moved to a new facility, the architects set up the men's and women's restrooms with the same number of stalls, and thus the same amount of toilet paper to be apportioned each day. However, the offices that were sent to the new facility tended to be disproportionately populated by women. This in turn meant that by about 2 p.m. each day, the women's rooms had run out of toilet paper. This lead to packs of desperate women raiding the men's rooms in search of their extra TP. Other women resorted to bringing their own, with rolls stacked up in their cubicles. Oh, the humanity!)

// ⊕ //

Question: What is the official policy for dressing up for Halloween?

Official Response: General dress code policy states that directorates and office directors establish dress standards, either traditional business or business casual, based on appropriate work attire for the duties and responsibilities of the work being performed. Additionally, they will ensure that their employees' work attire conforms to the established dress code for their office. Managers and supervisors will ensure that employees adhere to the dress standards established by the directorates and offices.

From a security perspective, please be advised: with the Halloween season coming up there are several offices that will be hosting Halloween functions. To this end, you should NOT wear a mask or have on character make-up when you enter or pass through the security checkpoints. All of the police officers manning the gate(s) would like to know that your face matches the one on your ID card. We do not have on file any Frankensteins, Broom Hildas, or Raggedy Anns, so we are sure that there is no badge to match those faces. Fake knives, guns, etc., are not permitted, so all of you buccaneers and pirates please assume that you're a land lubber for the day.

Subject to directorate and office guidance, you will be able to put on your costume, make-up, or mask when you get to the building. After you have donned your costume you must display your ID badge as is required of all employees and it should not be hidden by your costume.

Employee responses included:
- I want to see someone brief the directorate at the 7:30 meeting wearing a hook and an eye patch and talking like a pirate.
- I hate to nitpick, but Frankenstein was the Doctor and the Monster was the Green Guy.

I have been observing the behaviors of employees streaming in and out of the front entrance to the headquarters building for the past few days and noticed the following behavior. At least 85% of employees frequently use the handicapped button to keep the doors open. Once the doors are opened automatically, a long line would either file in or out. It seems that those are not willing to exert physical energy to actually manually open the doors. When I opened the doors, the doors are heavy to open, hence the tendency for employees to use the handicapped button. Are there any plans in the works to remedy this?

One poster replied: Instead of doors, we'll have strands of beads that everyone can mysteriously walk through every morning.

// 🌐 //

From the Splash Page announcements: AEREON Alerting Replacement Program = AARP. Please institute process to review program names and acronyms for new NSG projects and programs. Everyone in the US of A already knows what AARP is, and it is NOT the AEREON Alerting Replacement Program. The usage of that acronym for an NSG activity does not pass the laugh test, and will expose the program, its developers, and the NSG as a whole to ridicule. Not to mention comments from Congress that if NGA employees are already retired, then why are they paying us salaries? Adult supervision in the process of naming things has been needed for years.

Acronyms are supposed to provide a short-hand way to describe an activity in place of a long wordy phrase that takes up to much room on paper or too long to say in conversation. They need to be reasonably unique and not easily confused with other acronyms currently in use. The habit of using macho terms or action verbs as names for activities, with a name to justify that particular acronym being cobbled together afterwards also needs to be discouraged. The best way to do this is to have a group of people to run names and acronyms by before they become official to give them a smell/laugh test and not give the developer free reign (sic) to come up with silly things like AARP.

// 🌐 //

I wanted to let you know of an issue before it became a HUGE problem. The other day, I was eating lunch with some friends. We were sitting at the bar tables next to the glass elevators. I saw my friend's eyes open wide and looked to see what she was seeing. In the elevator, as it was rising, you can see right up the skirts of the ladies standing next to the glass inside the elevators. I immediately asked myself if I have ever worn a skirt/dress and taken those elevators. Is there a way to put some frosted material on the glass to about waist high? That's the only solution I could come up with. Do you have a better idea to mitigate this problem? I assure you that I will not be using those elevators on days I'm wearing a skirt/dress.

// 🌐 //

I was raised to believe that there was no such thing as a "stupid" question. Since the inception of this forum I no longer find this to be the case. In this economic climate many Americans would love to be in the position we find ourselves in. We have bigger issues to focus on than the extra hour or two that one has to wake up to get to work or that the Starbucks is getting our drink order wrong. I would like to thank you for your time and dedication to the workforce to answer all of the questions posed to you. I believe a vocal minority is being heard and the majority of the workforce is not only happy at NGA but proud to be a member of this Agency. I believe that the agency has its best years ahead and look forward to the ride. From a regular Band 3 average "Joe" employee I would like to say thank you for all you do for the workforce, the agency, and the IC as a whole. I am proud and thank to say that I work at NGA, for the DoD and for the IC. Again, this is just a simple thank you.

FOR SALE, ASTON MARTIN, SLIGHTLY USED

A subset of the social media fora is the plethora of For Sale boards. Most have straightforward wares to sell, but some do so in an entertaining manner, as seen below:

Wanted: Parts needed: Building a Spaceship! Captain Planet saved the world from 2012, now he needs your help to save the galaxy. I take your old computers, electronics, batteries, appliances, and car parts. No TVs. The parts will be recycled into a new spaceship. And remember: "the Power is YOURS!"

// ⊕ //

Decorative Samurai Swords. 3 of them. I have no idea why I have them, I don't even know why someone would make them. Three decorative Japanese swords on a display stand. They're 3 different sizes. They look neat, but I have no use for them. $100.

// ⊕ //

14-carat white gold diamond bridal ring with one princess cut diamond and 2 baguette cut accent stones. Retails $1,425.00. Natural princess cut diamond: clarity: I1 Color: G (near colorless) Natural baguette diamonds: Clarity: SI-1—SI-2 Color: F-G (near colorless) Ring size is 8 ½. Ring is in near perfect condition as it was worn infrequently.

// 🌐 //

Harry Potter e-books now available. My daughter just called and if you are a Harry Potter fan and have an e-reader, they are available. You can purchase the entire set for $99 or individually for $7.99.

- *Response 1:* Small correction: individual e-books are priced between $7.99 and $9.99; the entire set is available for $57.54 ($99 for 7 eight-dollar e-books would not be much of a deal.)
- *Response 2:* It would be if the government purchased them!

// 🌐 //

In response to an ad for a pot-bellied pig, one wag mimicked all of the language in an attempt to get rid of her out-of-shape hubby:

Large Pot-Belly Man Seeking Loving Home

My name is Hans. I am a loveable house-pig that enjoys sitting in a recliner or sleeping till noon. My favorite snacks are beer, meat, and beer. I am practicing very hard with my bathroom habits and hope to perfect them soon! I get along well with my brothers, even though they are dogs...but I like to chase cats.

At 40 years old, Hans weighs about 290 pounds and is due to reach a maximum of 350 pounds.

Hans's wife and food supplier recently came to her senses. There is no one in the house all day long, so he needs to go to a home which can provide lots of food, a recliner, and a remote.

Hans is neutered and up-to-date on most of his vaccines. (He may need a tetanus shot.) He comes with a bottle of Rumpleminz, good for the next two days that protects against bad breath and boredom.

Hans comes with his cooler, back scratcher, Marlin Perkins tranquilizer dart gun (needed for football season), any food or beer we have left, carrier, leash and harness (bow chica bow wow), his favorite stuffed animal and his favorite Eagles attire. We will pay $500 to someone to remove Hans and his accessories from our home. Hans resides a few miles north of scenic Collinsville, an easy drive from nowhere.

// 🌐 //

One especially unfortunate incomplete cut & paste posting offered:
> For Sale: Children and Adult
> Body
> Adult size is white for 40.00
> 2 Children size (for 8/9 year olds) 25.00 each
> Pink Kick Boxing Gloves 20.00

The responses included:
- The children seem a bit expensive given the upkeep and all, but if you can drop the cost on the gloves $5 we may have some room to negotiate.
- I'm suspicious about the adult. I'd have to see it, and perhaps run it through a few chores to see if this is really a value deal. I'm not saying "no", I just want to do a little homework first.
- I'm not sure I want to buy children…mine drive me darn near insane.
- I assume the adult is female by the pink adult gloves mentioned. I could take the adult off your hands as long as all the shots are up to date and she has a sweet temperament around the kids. Let me know.
- Can't NGA purchase these humans? Seems like free range humans would be a perfect addition to the wildlife reserve at NCE.
- NGA could acquire them, but they'd be instantly laid off. I know I'm supposed to say "furlough", but to me that word smacks of misdirection, like "pre-owned" instead of "used".
- The problem with free-range humans is they are likely to establish a nest in the parking lot, meaning at least 6 spaces roped off and unusable.
- I assume the missing word is "guards"…bodyguards. Seems like a steal, and the kickboxing gloves will protect their hands from harm while they're taking out anyone who tries to mess with me.

// ⊕ //

Finally, Bond could park his Aston Martin anywhere. Not so for those at DIA, who participated in this discussion of every real spy's greatest concern: parking:

Parking—Is that a spot? Nope!

Picture this—you're driving through the parking lot or the garage with hopes of finding a legal parking spot. You approach another row of cars, and you think you see an open spot down there. Although you haven't seen an open parking spot in ages, you've nearly forgotten what it looks like. However, you quickly turn down this row while looking around to make sure no one else gets there first. Then just as you start to turn the wheel into the space, there it is—hope dashed—as you see a tiny car parked in the space. You begin to ponder if you could share the space with this car; maybe no one would notice your car hanging out into the aisle. Hum, you quickly realize that's a bad idea. With your head hanging low, you continue your search for a parking space. Drivers of tiny cars—please help us out. Can you please not pull all the way into the parking space?

This generated the following series of replies:

- Since we're on the topic of tiny cars, drivers are reminded they are not permitted to bring tiny cars into the SCIF (*Ed's note:* SCIFs are secure facilities where one can create, work with, and store classified materials.)
- Ahhh. And I just so love to bring mine in. It fits me so well within my trench coat pocket.
- Yes, most tiny cars these days can be plugged into your USB port, which is clearly in violation of information security rules.
- Actually, it would be nice if we could all have the car that George Jetson drove to work. It would fit nicely into our briefcase and we wouldn't have any parking issues here at DIA Headquarters.
- Are there any cars that are "too smart"?
- KITT.
- I'd settle for smart drivers over smart cars any day.

- Are there any plans to upgrade the lockers outside the SCIFs to accommodate tiny cars.
- I dunno about lockers for tiny cars. Imagine how much you'd be irritated if you walked all the way to the parking lot and Then realized you'd left your tiny car back in the building. Man!

WHATEVER HAPPENED TO SHAKEN, NOT STIRRED?

Intelligence officers changed greatly in the 50 years since the release of the first James Bond film. This review of the favorite beverage of intelligence officers graced a blog:

- I ordered a tall Café Mocha at 0745 Central Daylight Time on 1 November in the year of our Lord 2012.
- I judged the service to be comparable to that of a standalone franchise or corporate Starbucks coffee house. The lady who took my order is the supervisor from Treat America, who was dressed professionally and appropriately in a part of smart black trousers, an aquamarine blouse and a black cardigan sweater. It took approximately 7 minutes and 16 seconds from completion of my order to when I had a reasonably hot premium coffee beverage in my hand (more on that to follow). The beverage tasted good and consistent with the flavor profile of a Café Mocha. The Café Mocha cost $3.57 with tax, which is slightly less than standalone Starbucks coffee houses, of which a Tall Café Mocha costs between $3.72-$3.96 depending on the local tax rate.

- The Café Mocha was much sweeter than its standalone Starbucks brethren. With sucrose being the reference and at a value of 1.00, I would assess this Café Mocha to have a sweetness value of approximately 1.17 to 1.25 depending on the sensitivity of one's sweetness receptors resident in the taste buds. My advice to those who desire a more true to form Starbucks Café Mocha should order their beverage with 1 to 2 less pumps of mocha flavoring or request less chocolate syrup drizzled on the whipped cream. In addition, the Café Mocha was slightly cold as I returned to my cubicle. With typical Starbucks Café Mochas, it takes approximately 4 to 5 minutes for the beverage to reach optimal drinking temperature. When I waited that time with the We Proudly Serve beverage, it was approximately 5 to 7 degrees cooler than it should be.

- In my professional opinion, I would frequent this We Proud Serve establishment again and will most likely return within a 1 to 2 week period. Analyst Comment: As the baristas become more comfortable and thus, more proficient, in the creation of premium Starbucks coffee beverages, I assess their taste to slide closer to the Starbucks "standard". The next time I order a Café Mocha, I will request one less pump of mocha flavoring and a temperature of 160 Fahrenheit.

- The overall quality as reminiscent of Starbucks and actually exceeded my expectation. I fully expect that as the baristas gain more experience in the craft of brewing and serving fine premium coffee beverages, the quality will continue to improve until it reaches the lofty Starbucks gold standard.

Any questions can be directed to the undersigned.

Faithfully submitted,

{name sanitized}
PREMIUM COFFEE BEVERAGE ENTHUSIAST

Speaking of coffee, one wag collected "You know you've had enough coffee when" jokes, including:

- You answer the door before the people knock.
- You speed walk in your sleep.
- All your kids are named Joe.
- You haven't blinked since the last lunar eclipse.
- You lick the coffeepot clean.
- You spend a vacation visiting "Maxwell House".
- You're the employee of the month at the local coffeehouse, but you don't work there.
- The nurse needs a scientific calculator to take your pulse.
- Your T-shirt says: "Decaf is the devil's blend."
- You've worn out the handle on your favorite mug.
- People get dizzy just watching you.
- You're offended when people use the word "brew" to mean beer.
- You have a picture of the caffeine molecule on your coffee mug.
- You don't even remember your second cup.
- Your first aid kit is a pint of coffee and an I.V. hookup.
- You don't wait for the water to boil anymore.
- You go to AA meetings for the free coffee.
- Your two cats are named "Cream" and "Sugar".
- You introduce your spouse as your "coffeemate".

DRESS CODES

The Office of the Director of National Intelligence informally orchestrated the creation of a burn bag tie (using the red and white stripes on a light brown background that is found on typical burn bags) for the International Brotherhood of United Stealworkers.

Cultural clashes between generations and various subcultures come to the fore in various ways of expressing individuality and in-group identity through sartorial splendor. CIA officers often knew that summertime was upon us when the annual Executive Director's memo on standards of dress was issued, with the aggressively casual styles of the summer interns in mind. NGA officers shared the ExDir's concerns, posting the following observations on their internal social media:

I was wondering if there any plan to implement a dress code at NGA West? There has been a steady and rapid decline in the professional or even business dress code of the past 2 years. I have seen individuals wear tie-dye flannel pajama pants to work, every day. The youngest workers believe that jeans are appropriate for every day of the week and that hats are ok to be worn inside, sometimes wearing them backwards. (*Compiler's note:* It's been my belief that you lose an apparent 30 IQ points by wearing a ball cap any way other than how the brim was meant to be used—in front, to shade your eyes from the sun!) Some of the young ladies here are wearing clothing that is more appropriate for a bar rather than going to work. (*Compiler's note:* Hey, buddy, stop tryin' to ruin it for the rest of us!) I can only imagine the perception of other agencies must have of us when they visit our facilities. It's truly disappointing that our workforce is not held to even a reasonable standard.

// ⊕ //

Are there homeless people here at NGE? On any given day, it's nearly impossible to avoid seeing two types of "homeless"-looking people walking the halls. It is embarrassing. The first group has the destitute look, typically wearing an oversized shirt/top, sweatpants, and sneakers. (These people are not en route to the gym.) The second group brings the chic homeless look, wearing the designer label shirts/sweaters/tops, jeans, and shoes that bring purposeful (and expensive) informality and indifference. All this points to the need for a clear and enforced dress code. We all claim to be professionals. Will we dress as such?

// ⊕ //

I was wondering if there is/has been any consideration about addressing the level of professionalism of our workforce. As I walk through the Atrium and halls of NGA Headquarters, I see more and more folks dressing down during the week and even saw one of the presenters at the 0830 meeting wearing a polo shirt. I'm sure I'll be labeled as someone "living in the past," but I remember when people took pride in being an IC professional and carried themselves as such. You don't see this kind of behavior at the other agencies and I can't help but think this has an impact on how we're viewed across the Community.

// ⊕ //

How should we in NSA accessorize around a Blue Badge? (*Ed's note:* Staff officers in the Intelligence Community wear blue-framed badges; contractors wear green-framed ones.) I am reaching out for male and female fashion advice for those seeking modern professional attire in uncontrollable environmental elements. Such elements might include florescent lighting, lack of sunlight, and drab hallways with uncouth furniture. Some accessories might include a blue or green badge strung around the neck and a blue canvas courier bag. We don't dress for success. We dress

for mission-critical success. Here are a few answers, depending upon the organization in which you work:
- If S1 and/or D, a charcoal modern-fit three-piece with matching leather belt and shoes.
- If S2, tan chinos with and a fitted plaid or striped dress shirt with matching leather belt and shoes.
- If S31, straight-fit jeans and a fitted polo with matching leather belt and shoes.
- If S31114, straight-fit jeans and a fitted t-shirt with matching canvas belt and shoes.
- If S32, straight-fit jeans and a fitted hacker t-shirt with green hair and matching canvas belt and shoes.
- If F6, dress as your cover and/or Band.
- If F5, dress for the deployment and/or Band.
- If IAD, dress as our industry partners and/or Band.
- If ADET (*Ed's note:* training staff), dress better than your students.
- If NSA police officer, wear your uniform.
- If Dog (*Ed's note:* canine) employee, keep fur clean and combed, unless taking down a baddie.
- If Sodexho (*Ed's note:* cafeteria staff), dress in purple, red, black and a smile.
- If military, dress in your service uniform if permitted.

// //

Analysts generally keep spare clothes—at least a suit jacket, pressed shirt, and tie—in case they're called downtown (this usually means the White House, but can also refer to Congress, State, and other locales across the Potomac) unexpectedly. My colleague avoided potential embarrassment by having a full ensemble ready the morning the President showed up and wanted to personally meet the authors of the pieces written for him. She'd apparently learned from a friend who briefed the Agency Director in a nice suit and flip flops.

// //

While we as an office purchased the "office sport coat" from a local Goodwill store ($3.50) initially as a joke pushing back against our management who was trying to enforce a non-existent dress code, the "OS" has come in handy a number of times. The neat thing is, since it's a brown/gold/black checked sport coat that can fit the second biggest guy in the office, it pretty much goes with anything, including polo shirts or the Don Johnson-esque mock turtleneck. The OS has now become a bit of a tradition for the guys (and one girl) to wear to inconsequential award photos with the branch chief or O-5 with a certificate.

// 🌐 //

I once briefed the Chief of Staff of the Air Force with my nametag on the wrong side. Lesson learned: set up your uniform the night before, not at 1 a.m. when you get up to brief at 5 a.m.

// 🌐 //

I don't know if it's easier or not for women to keep emergency attire at the office. I'll be honest and admit that my emergency personal gear consists of a hairbrush, extra shirt and antiperspirant (hey—sometimes waking up at 3 in the morning means you forget certain things!).

I'm sure I'm not the only analyst out there who has been so absorbed thinking about one particular problem set or another that I have no cognitive powers to spare for things like…I dunno…getting dressed in the morning?

My lack of emergency attire has resulted in some pretty bold fashion statements, if I may say so myself (hey, it's been corroborated by multiple sources). I have no intention of ever again being caught dead in pinstriped pants and a polka-dotted tie.

Add in the occasional mismatched socks, absent belt, or clashing tie, and you've got an entirely preventable reputation as either an aspiring fashion visionary or someone whose mother/wife/other significant influence never taught them to dress themselves. Or maybe that's just me?

// 🌐 //

One recent visitor to my building had a black polo shirt on with a logo and in government-style block letters the phrase "Roswell Denial Team".

FURLOUGH THIS

The 2013 sequestration and attendant furloughs of many federal workers brought out several ideas on cost saving solutions to avoid furloughs for federal employees:
- Cafeterias will be shut down. Only lukewarm gruel will be served. Employees must provide their own bowls/plates and silverware.
- All lighting will be shut off, including emergency lighting. Employees may bring in flashlights if they choose. (*Employee's comment:* A few years ago, the NRO unscrewed every-other lightbulb in most ceiling lights.)
- Elevators will be shut down.
- Air conditioning and heating will be shut down. Employees are encouraged to dress appropriately.
- Federal employees will be required to bring their own toilet paper. (This point is irrelevant because bathroom breaks are prohibited.) (*Ed's note:* During the first months of a new building in which I worked, there was a toilet paper crisis.

The designers had figured that there should be as many women's stalls as men's stalls in the restrooms. Unfortunately, the offices assigned to this building were populated overwhelmingly by women. This in turn meant a run—please excuse that one—on women's restroom stalls. By 2 p.m. each day, the women's rooms had run out of toilet paper. In some cases, this led to women staking out the men's rooms, and conducting clandestine raids for toilet paper. In other cases, women began bringing their own stashes of TP, keeping them at the ready at their office desks. The office soon had the decorative cachet of a Costco. History does not record when, how—or even whether—this problem was solved.)

- There will be one computer per 10 employees. Fights over computer time will serve as an alternate method of RIF (reduction in force).
- Water service to the buildings will be shut off. Employees are encouraged to bring their own daily water supply.
- As trash service will also be terminated, employees will be encouraged to take home any trash they produce during the day.
- All sick leave is hereby cancelled. Sick employees are to report to the cafeterias for work.
- Employees may earn extra income ($0.25/hour) working the basement sweat shop producing widgets. 12-hour shifts (no breaks) and 6 days/week minimum required.
- Non-essential furniture (read: chairs) will be auctioned off. Employees may Not purchase a chair in the auction.
- But hey, you'll still have a job!

Still other employees suggested sequestration-themed tee-shirts, including:

- I survived sequestration.
- The person in charge of that is on furlough.
- Nonessential
- Furlough: taking one for the team.
- Don't ask me. I've been furloughed.
- Bros Before Furloughs.
- Will furlough notices be printed on recycled paper?
- I got 99 problems but a job ain't one.
- I want to hear Alicia Keys sing "This girl is for hiiiiiiiire!"
- Furlough: Because cutting my salary 20% for 6 months is totally going to get the country out of debt.
- Furlough: Because a federal employee's mortgage payments aren't as important as a Social Security recipient's greens fees.
- NGA Furlough Policy: We care about our employees in this time of hardship; that's why we're suspending alternative work schedules for no apparent reason.
- (inspired by the movie Argo) Furlough F#$% yourself.

Even if you're furloughed, you can still leave an out-of-office message:

- I am currently furloughed and unable to respond to your e-mail. If this were a weekend or a holiday I would respond to your e-mail on my Blackberry, but federal employees are not permitted to use their BBs or perform any work on furlough days. Your national security is important to me. Please leave a message and I will get back with you tomorrow.

- Thank you for your message. Due to unexpectedly high volume of incompetence, intransigence, and irresponsibility by the elected leadership of this great country, we are experiencing 20 percent delays. Please hold until a public servant is available to assist you. Your e-mail will be answered in the order it was received. Thank you.

- Furloughed! In case of emergency please contact the Senate Appropriate Committee at 202-224-7363 and request supplemental funding. I will return your call as soon as possible.

- Today's my furlough day. I am supposed to do 20 percent less work. You'll find out on Monday whether your e-mail is part of the other 80 percent.

- It's against the law for me to check my Blackberry today, so I'm going to the beach instead.

As if sequestration was not bad enough, a dispute between the White House and certain factions in Congress led to a partial government shutdown in October 2013. Observations among those members of the IC who were sent home included:

- **Furlough week one:** YAHOO! Week vacation!
- **Furlough week two:** Sweet! Another week.
- **Furlough week three:** Jeez, getting a little nervous here…
- **Furlough week four:** Getting bored. Are the two sides talking yet?
- **Furlough week five:** Broke and smelly. When are we going back to work?
- **Furlough week six:** Living on government cheese. No money for beer.
- **Furlough week seven:** HELP ME! Starting to hear voices inside my head.
- **Furlough week eight:** Got a part-time job as a Walmart greeter: "May I put a smiley face sticker on your shirt?"

ENGAGEMENT CODES

Virtually every military organization you can name has an intelligence organization, which abides by the rules of its parent component, including:

MARINE CORPS RULES:
1. Be courteous to everyone, friendly to no one.
2. Decide to be aggressive enough, quickly enough.
3. Have a plan.
4. Have a back-up plan, because the first one probably won't work.
5. Be polite. Be professional. But, have a plan to kill everyone you meet.
6. Do not attend a gunfight with a handgun whose caliber does not start with a '4.'
7. Anything worth shooting is worth shooting twice. Ammo is cheap. Life is expensive.
8. Move away from your attacker. Distance is your friend. Lateral & diagonal preferred.
9. Use cover or concealment as much as possible.
10. Flank your adversary when possible. Protect yours.

11. Always cheat; always win. The only unfair fight is the one you lose.
12. In 10 years no one will remember details of caliber, stance, or tactics. They'll only remember who lived.
13. If you are not shooting, you should be communicating your intention to shoot.
14. To err is human, to forgive divine. Neither of which is Marine Corps policy.

Navy SEAL Rules:
1. Look very cool in sunglasses.
2. Kill every living thing within view.
3. Adjust Speedo.
4. Check hair in mirror.

US Army Rangers Rules:
1. Walk 50 miles wearing 75 pound rucksack while starving.
2. Locate individuals requiring killing.
3. Request permission via radio from 'Higher' to perform killing.
4. Curse bitterly when mission is aborted.
5. Walk out 50 miles wearing a 75 pound rucksack while starving.

US Army Rules:
1. Curse bitterly when receiving operational order.
2. Make sure there is extra ammo and extra coffee.
3. Curse bitterly.
4. Curse bitterly.
5. Do not listen to 2nd LTs; it can get you killed.
6. Curse bitterly.

US Air Force Rules:

1. Have a cocktail.
2. Adjust temperature on air-conditioner.
3. See what's on HBO.
4. Ask 'What is a gunfight?'
5. Request more funding from Congress with a 'killer' PowerPoint presentation.
6. Wine & dine "key' Congressmen, invite DOD & defense industry executives.
7. Receive funding, set up new command and assemble assets.
8. Declare the assets 'strategic' and never deploy them operationally.
9. Hurry to make 13:45 tee-time.
10. Make sure the base is as far as possible from the conflict but close enough to have tax exemption.

US Navy Rules:

1. Go to Sea.
2. Drink Coffee.
3. Deploy Marines

DI STYLIN'

The Night Before Christmas (edited for DI Style)

(This is a good first draft but would benefit from revisions to clarify messages, draw out US implications, and tighten prose. Make sure message is clear in title and lead sentence.)

<u>All the creatures were still on Christmas Eve</u>

~~'Twas the night before Christmas, when all through the house~~

~~Not a creature was stirring, not even a mouse.~~

The stockings were hung by the chimney with care,

In hopes that St. Nicholas soon would be there;

The children were nestled all snug in their beds,

Vision of <u>candy</u> ~~sugar plums~~ *(jargon)* danced in their heads;

And mamma in her 'kerchief, and I in my cap,

Had just settled down for a long winter's nap

When out on the lawn there arose such a clatter,

I hurried to the window and opened it. ~~I sprang from the bed to see what was the matter. Away to the window I flew like a flash.~~ *(too wordy)*

Tore open the shutters and threw up the sash.

The moon on the breast of the new-fallen snow

Gave the ~~lustre~~ luster *(use US spelling)* of mid-day *(no hyphen)* to objects below.

When, what to my wondering eyes should appear,

But a miniature sleigh, and eight tiny reindeer *(Is this credible? Describe source)*

With a little old driver, so lively and quick,

I knew in a moment it must be St. Nick.

More rapid than eagles *(how rapid? Be specific)* his coursers they came,

And he whistled, and shouted, and called them by name,

~~Now Dasher! Now, Dancer, now, Prancer and Vixen!~~

~~On, Comet! On Cupid! On, Donder and Blitzen!~~ *(move details to backgrounder)*

TO the top of the porch! To the top of the wall!

Now dash away! ~~Dash away! Dash away all!~~ *(redundant)*

As ~~dry~~ leaves that before the wild hurricane fly,

When they meet with an obstacle, mount to the sky.

So up to the house-top the coursers they flew,

With the sleigh full of toys, and St. Nicholas, too.

And then, in a twinkling, I heard on the roof *(Is this plausible on a pitched roof?)*

The prancing and pawing of each little hoof. *(Did source hear this himself?)*

As I drew in my head, and was turning around,

~~Down the chimney~~ St. Nicholas came down the chimney with a bound.

He was dressed all in fur, ~~from his head to his foot,~~ *(redundant)*

And his clothes were <u>dirty</u> ~~all tarnished with ashes and soot~~;
He had toys on his back ~~A bundle of toys he had flung on his back,~~
~~And he looked like a peddler just opening his pack.~~
~~His eyes—how they twinkled! His dimples how merry!~~
~~His cheeks were like roses, his nose like a cherry!~~
~~His droll little mouth was drawn up like a bow,~~
~~And the beard of his chin was as white as the snow.~~
~~The stump of a pipe he held tight in his teeth~~
~~Encircled his head like a wreath,~~
~~Face and a little round belly,~~
~~That shook when he laughed like a bowlful of jelly.~~
~~He was chubby and plump, a right jolly old elf.~~
(All these details could be moved to a facing page graphic. Also please resolve contradiction between "little" belly and "plump." Perhaps these are from different sources?)

And I laughed when I saw him ~~in spite of myself~~
<u>His movements were nonthreatening.</u> ~~A wink of his eye and a twist of his head,~~
~~Soon gave me to know I had nothing to dread.~~
He spoke not a word, but went straight to his work,
And filled all the stockings, then turned with a jerk.
~~And laying his finger aside of his nose,~~
~~Then~~ <u>And</u> giving a nod, up the chimney he rose *(What do we know about the source's mental condition?)*
He sprang to his sleigh, to his team gave a whistle,
And away they all flew ~~like the down of a thistle~~
But I heard him say ~~exclaim, ere~~ <u>before</u> *(archaic)* he drove away out of sight
"~~Happy~~ <u>Merry</u> Christmas (US style) to all, and to all a good-night"

(Generally well said! However, what factors will determine whether St. Nicholas will return next year, and, if so, what sort of toys will he bring? Signposts to help the reader? Are there opportunities for policymakers to influence the outcome?)

// ⊕ //

A Letter to Santa, DI-Style

Dear Santa: *(Should this be Santa Claus? More specific/less prone to confusion)*

This is Timmy, Brian, and Becky. <u>You must be surprised</u>. *(How do you purport to know how Santa feels? A logic assertion would work better: "You have good reason to be surprised…")* ~~that~~ we are writing to you this year, ~~since~~ because it's been a while *(please be more specific! List the number of years.) (Second editor: I disagree. It's OK to be general here.)* since any of us has written you ~~a letter, but~~ *(new sentiment, so new sentence).* ~~w~~We wanted to wish you and Mrs. Santa Claus a ~~merry~~ good ~~c~~Christmas *(Second editor: I'd suggest "joyous". "Good" is rather general—specifically, we're talking about "joy" here.)* We have been ~~really~~ good this year. We share a room well, play well with others, and work really hard at school. *(More specifically, at the Kent School.)* <u>We wanted to make sure that you knew what we want for Christmas.</u> *(Vague. Why not "We judge it important that you appreciate what we want as gifts from you this year.")*

Timmy: Would ~~really like~~ value Internet access, longer lunch breaks, and a cruise *(Is it important to consider where Timmy would like to go? Something to think about.)*

Brian: ~~Would really like~~ requires an even bigger house, a new car, and ~~more~~ greater quantities and quality coffee for the ~~Kent School~~ IATP's use. *(Is Brian more concerned with IATP than the greater Kent School? Something to think about.)*

Becky: Wishes to ~~go to~~ attend the IAF *(First time used, so spell out International Association of Facilitators)* conference in Denver <u>in March</u>. In addition, please ensure snow. She would like her ~~SAS, 15,~~ a raise; and she would really like to sit by a window ~~for the rest of her career~~ forever.

~~Thank you, Santa, for bringing us toys.~~ We have high confidence that you will bring us toys, and this will almost certainly cause us to be grateful.

~~Sincerely~~ *("Warm Regards" works better)*
Timmy W.-Y-, Brian G., and Becky S.

// ⊕ //

The following prank edition of a spot report made the rounds during the Libya crisis in April 2011. The linguistic flourishes reflect that a change in generational style has taken place:

Middle East and North Africa Situation Report, 1 April 2011, 2500 EDT

SUPER, REALLY SECRET//AC/DC//ORC/HOBBIT

(Footnote: This report was prepared by the Presidential Support Advisors, CIA. Accolades and offers of food may be presented directly in person to the table. You know the one.)

Libya

Military Developments

Fighting continued yesterday in select Libyan cities over Lady Gaga's "Born this Way" World Tour concert tickets, according to Anderson "The Silver Fox" Cooper, reporting. CNN and BBC reports indicate that fighting was over some other stuff, too.

- According to psychic readings by Miss Cleo, pro-Qadhafi forces on 29 March killed a bunch of people using "what the spirits tell me might have been guns." This has been confirmed by clandestine sources, who say it was "definitely guns."
- According to a clandestine source claiming firsthand access, stuff is blowing up. Like, forrealz blowing up. That was totally a piece of shrapnel that just flew by. Why am I still reporting when I should be taking cover? I am not being paid enough for this s***.

- Analysts predict the war between pro-regime forces and the Axis of Good—made up of the United States, the United Kingdom, Borneo, Mongolia, Bill Gates, and Oprah—is likely to last awhile. Or maybe not.

Political Activity

Libyan Army officers in late March remarked that Libyan leader Qadhafi was likely hunkered down in a Tripoli safehaven trying to out-Charlie Sheen former Two and a Half Men star Charlie Sheen, according to a clandestine source with second-hand access. His attempt to find two porn star "Goddesses" on Craigslist so far has not yielded results, however, according to press reports.
- CIA analysts remain divided as to whether he has had plastic surgery or not. Qadhafi, not Sheen.

The Qadhafi regime is still working to convince the international community that regime forces are not involved in military action against rebel-controlled cities, saying, quote, "You misunderstand. We are playing duck-duck-goose. Ha ha."
- Regime leadership as of mid-March was evaluating whether the international community would believe that opposition war casualties were "just faking it," according to Moldovan intelligence. Tripoli was also considering declaring Benghazi a "Zombie Disaster Zone" to justify Libyan military action against the city.

International Reaction

France is preparing to be invaded, according to the French press.
- "We're always getting invaded," whined a spokesman for Paris late last night.

Arabian Peninsula

Oman. Analysts would like to point out that the Sultan's name is Qaboos. Ka-boos.

Qatar. The US Embassy in Doha reports that Qatar will most likely remain one of the region's most stable governments, but analysts assess that the country is so small that, like, four people with sticks could single-handedly take it over. Seriously.

Elsewhere in the Region

Syria. An official close to President Asad told the US Ambassador last week that Asad really, really wants political and economic reforms, but that to do so would limit his absolute control of power so.

- Probably in an effort to head off the growing protest movement, a spokesman for Damascus announced that in the future the government would kill anyone who protested. President Asad later clarified that the spokesman was kidding. But not really.

Tunisia. Would like to remind people that it totally started this whole Arab revolution thing. Focus, people, focus!

// ⊕ //

Leadership analysts—those who follow the activities and decisions of world leaders—offered their own spoofs in 1993:

World Leadership Notes

- **Yel'tsin** passing out pork rinds at Constitutional Conference...planning summit with Ukraine's Kravchuk, possibly next weekend, to discuss how to wangle invitations to Walkers Point, sail jointly to Kennebunkport using Black Sea Fleet.

- **Major** ready to give up on Maastricht treaty, apply for US annexation...legal experts advise him he may have to abrogate Treaty of Ghent, surrender to US in War of 1812 in order to legitimize the application.

- **Kohl** caught in major faux pas in visit to Ukraine this week...joked that he liked chicken in Kiev better than Turks in Germany...Genscher calling foul.

- **Mitterrand** weighing surgical enhancements to improve perceived image as a statesman...considering nose enlargement, additional de gall bladder implant...tiring of working with Socialist-led government; grumped to aide that if he must cohabit, it should be with Catherine Deneuve.

- **Ciampi** distracted by severe bout of eczema on hands... doctors blame it on keeping fingers crossed his name will not turn up in ever-widening scandal investigation.

- **Mulroney** looking into opening trading post on Meech Lake...will carry no goods made in Quebec.

- **Miyazawa** willing to open Japanese rice market to US imports if he gets exclusive contract as Japanese TV spokesperson for Uncle Ben's...Mitsubishi engineers already at work developing 30-second version of Minute Rice.

THE EDITORS STRIKE BACK

Editors at the *President's Daily Brief* don't cotton to no bad 'ritin'. Here are a few comments they left on papers that weren't quite ready for the Oval Office:

- This article should be pregnant with ideas because you have been screwing with it so long, but I can't understand a thing you have written.
- This is a well-written piece of shit.
- The paucity of analysis is only exceeded by the poorness of the writing.
- This draft should be shortened and broadened.
- Never has so many words been written to so little so poorly.
- A fart makes a better draft than this.
- This draft is unintelligible for its weak points.
- This is a turd.
- If I understood what you are saying, I would disagree violently.

- Seldom have I seen a paper that presents trivial ideas so eloquently (or vice-versa).
- I like the ending of the paper: it is a shame it could have come in the first paragraph.
- It is a joy to read a paper like this, it makes me feel so superior.
- I've gotten better stuff from between my toes.
- This draft started going downhill right after the title.
- I've seen better stuff than this in my kitty litter box.
- I really like the margins of this paper.
- I realize this paper was a struggle—it is a shame you lost.
- To the victor goes the spoils: if we can find a victor, I think we have the spoils here.
- If this is supposed to provide food for thought, I think my mind is about to puke.

// ⊕ //

Humorists claimed that assessments referring to Moshe Dayan, who wore an eye patch, were classified "Secret, Eye Only".

// ⊕ //

The Prepositional Defense

Editorial excellence helped two FBI agents who had been caught engaging in, um, extracurricular collaboration during a holiday party. The couple discovered that they had lots, or at least lust, in common, and snuck off to an FBI official vehicle in the parking lot, where they engaged in enthusiastic collaboration. Security cameras caught all of the illicit goings-on. Authorities knew that something wasn't right, and had to find some kind of offense with which to charge the duo. They settled on abuse of government property. The editorial skills of the couple came in handy, though, when they successfully argued that they had been caught on the vehicle, not in it. The former would have constituted the violation, the latter would not.

Platt's Law

The oddities of DI editorial culture were presaged by its CIA predecessors. As an editor for a decade, I often counseled new analysts that the key to getting published what you want is determined by the number of editors—odd or even—that you face. The first editor will change your analysis 180 degrees. The second editor, under pressure to establish his/her usefulness, will change his colleague's prose exactly 180 degrees—back to what the analyst originally wrote.

Demonstrating that there is nothing new under the sun—or at least in my humor writing—*Studies in Intelligence* reported that "All old-time analysts in the profession have heard of Platt's Law; few are familiar with its exact terms. Like Darwin's theory of evolution, it has often been distorted or misrepresented, giving rise to grave errors. For the guidance of the young we publish herewith the original formulation of this seminal discovery, as recently exhumed from ancient files.

25 August 1951

Mr. Sherman Kent
Office of National Estimates, CIA

My dear Mr. Kent:

As one of the earliest purchasers and most constant readers of your classic on "Strategic Intelligence," I am writing to invite your attention to the omission from your (otherwise) excellent book of a fundamental principle in the production of intelligence.

Assume the following situation:

1. You have prepared after much thought and wide discussion the first draft of an Intelligence Estimate. This draft contains certain details and statements which your careful study of the problem leads you to believe should be included.

2. This first draft is reviewed by the first echelon above your own. Members of this echelon read your details. After thus getting the benefit

of your explanations, they find these details self-evident and so eliminate them from the paper along with many of your other pet phrases. So the second draft is prepared and stripped to the bare essentials.

3. The second higher echelon, on reviewing the second draft thus cut to the bone, finds many of the bare statements lacking in proper justification or background. This second echelon therefore insists on the inclusion of more explanation and details. So the third draft is prepared, restoring the details and pet explanatory phrases which echelon No. 1 cut out.

4. In turn, the next higher echelon reviewing this third draft and receiving the benefit of the explanations now once more included, finds these details unnecessary and cuts them out. ...

5. And so on, from echelon of review to echelon of review ad infinitum.

General Principle derived from the above universal experience:

Whether or not the necessary explanatory details and pet phrases of an intelligence paper appear in the paper as finally published, depends entirely upon whether the number of higher groups which successively review the paper is even or odd respectively.

I have, Sir, the honor to be your humble follower in the study of fundamental intelligence principles,

Washington PLATT
Brigadier General USAR-Hon.

one-time AC of S, G2 Armored Force
"AC of S, G-2 XIX Corps in ETO
Commanding General 98th Infantry Division
now Lower echelon Intelligence Officer, OSI-CIA"

Ed's Note: Platt's Law became part of the lore of Agency analysts' social psychological principles handed down over the years. These unwritten rules were eventually collected for *Studies in Intelligence* by Charles D. Cremeans in his "Basic Psychology for Intelligence Analysts", not to be confused with the seminal book by my former officemate, Richards Heuer, *The Psychology of Intelligence Analysis*.

Basic Psychology for Intelligence Analysts: Some Rules, Ploys, and Plays

When Allen Dulles chose to have the words *"For ye shall know the truth and the truth shall make you free,"* carved in white marble at the entrance to the Headquarters building he was giving expression to an article of faith in the intelligence profession. We must believe that knowledge of the truth sustains and supports our government or we couldn't justify what we are doing.

Working intelligence officers know, however, that it isn't always as easy as it sounds. "What is the truth? How much evidence do you have to have? How selected? How organized? How presented? How evaluated before we have the truth that will make our country free? And free from what? We all know that good and true men disagree on these matters, as on the evidence on any given subject of intelligence concern. We also know that from time to time, every intelligence officer worth his salt wakes up with a shock to realize that he has been misreading the evidence on some familiar topic. This can happen because he has gone along with the common wisdom, accepted unexamined assumptions, or just plain gotten into a rut. It can also happen if preoccupation with success, or mere survival in the intelligence culture become more important than intelligence itself.

The sensitive intelligence officer becomes aware from time to time of the effect on our finished product of the interaction of personalities and institutions within the Intelligence Community. We are, after all, human beings; we have deadlines to meet; we tend to favor our own conclusions over those of others; and we all know that a little salesmanship here and there, a little blarney, a measure of cajolery, and some basic psychology can often get a paper agreed to and on its way to the White House, while without such inputs it might languish and spoil under the heavy hands of some well meaning but less subtle colleagues.

The object of this paper is to look at some of the ways in which we get our work done, ways that depend more on human psychology than on cold reason. The purpose in mind is not to collect a bag of tricks, a primer of intelligencemanship, but to focus a spotlight on one aspect of our craft which is usually ignored. The purpose in doing this is not to suggest that an end be put to this kind of thing. God forbid that we stop being human, that we coldly reject, as being unsuited to our profession, such phenomena as the well-known eloquence of the distinguished dean of photointerpreters. But we should be aware of ourselves as we really are and not be misled into thinking all our peccadilloes foster the rapid and certain discovery of the truth.

We may start with a look at some of the oft quoted laws of intelligence.1 The most famous of these is Platt's Law, which reads, as set down by its discoverer: "Whether or not the necessary explanatory details and pet phrases of an intelligence paper appear in the paper as finally published, depends entirely upon whether the number of higher groups which successively review the paper is even or odd respectively."2 In the Office of National Estimates this is sometimes rendered: "If the Staff writes it long, the Board wants it short—and vice versa."

Another famous principle is that of Excessive Approval. Every intelligence Indian—i.e., drafter—knows that when the review board or panel, or whatever the higher echelon is, responds to a request for comments with unstinted praise, there comes a point at which the drafter feels a sense of foreboding. It usually means that his paper is about to be torn to shreds.

All veterans of intelligence coordination are familiar with the law of Emphasis by Place. This law is often referred to in this manner: "I suggest that the item referred to at the end of the paragraph—or section, or paper—be brought up to the beginning in order to give it greater emphasis." It is equally often cited by urging that an item that appears at the beginning be put at the end "in order to give it greater emphasis." Adjudication on this matter usually depends on whether the Chairman wants to argue about whether emphasis is bestowed by early or late reference or whether he thinks the time is suitable for a throwaway concession in the hope that the gesture can be collected on at a later time.

Most notorious of the laws of intelligence is Murphy's Law: *"When something can be misunderstood, it will be."* The archives contain no record of Murphy. He may have been an honorable and well-intentioned man, but, sad to say, his law is more often than not cited by someone whose opinion of his boss is that he can and will read only one sentence at a time. The result of this assumption is that all the supporting calculations and data must be stuffed into the sentence in question, making it incomprehensible by the most intelligent reader, and probably to the boss for whose benefit the re-writing is being proposed.

A quick look at these laws of intelligence shows that they really are techniques of persuasion rather than laws the knowledge of which enables one to understand the behavior of phenomena in the real world. In fact it is in the realm of persuasion—of others, as well, sometimes, as of ourselves—that psychology most often obtrudes into intelligence.

Almost every intelligence analyst learns that if he wants to play it safe, or if he just doesn't know what is going to happen, an easy way out may be found through the Continuation of Present Trends formula. Unless he runs into really bad luck, an intelligence analyst of modest competence can usually go through a career with good marks simply by summarizing the evidence, and then pronouncing thus: "present trends are likely to continue." When this gets boring or too conspicuous, the More and More formula is often called into use. "King Hussein will find it more and more difficult to maintain control ...," or he "will find it increasingly difficult. ..." This gets to be a problem when he has been finding it more and more, as well as increasingly difficult for years and years and still hangs on. Then it becomes increasingly difficult for the analyst. The point is not that he should be ashamed of himself for being unable to find an answer to King Hussein's future in all that mass of paper that flows across his desk but that it should be quite clear to himself and to his readers that the evidence doesn't provide the basis for much of a judgment—which, of course, he should go on looking for despite the inadequacies of information and insight.

Perhaps the fundamental relationship among intelligence officers is that between the expert and the nonexpert. The former, of course, being the person who is supposed to know—although he doesn't necessarily really know all about Patagonia just because he is on the desk—and the latter being the person who reviews, edits, revises, or just approves his work. We are talking, of course, about the Indian and the chief in the intelligence analysis tribal culture. In real life the expert is usually comparatively young and the nonexpert or supervisor, comparatively old. The supervisor was probably an expert once but has to cover too wide a field, has too much administrative responsibility, or is too tired to be anything but a "generalist."

Actually, both the specialist and the supervisor have essential jobs to do, but the relationship is inherently a difficult one and, as a consequence, the ingenuity of man (real "intelligence officers") rises to the challenge with formulae that make life easier—sometimes for one, sometimes for both parties. For the expert the neatest solution is to know so much, to calculate so well the requirements and the quirks of the supervisor as well as the supervisor's supervisor, and to translate this into such a good end-product that the boss can only sigh and sign off. Unfortunately, not every supervisor knows when he is getting a perfect draft, and so even the best of the experts resort to certain stratagems to make their lives tolerable.

One approach, very often overdone, is that of laying on the expertise with a trowel: "Well, you know sir, unless you have lived with the Khmers as I have it is quite impossible to understand their reaction to the current situation." Another frequently used ploy is that of drowning your opponent, or boss, with facts. One famous "expert," who did know as much about the Arabs as anyone in town, insisted on going into the fine points of tribal differences, whatever the issue at hand, until in the end he had only to open his mouth to provoke groans and numerous visits to the washroom. In the first case by taking the line that only experts can understand, and in the second, by becoming irrelevant, the expert weakens his position and, indeed emphasizes the need for the intervention of a nonexpert, preferably one with good sense and judgment.

For his part the nonexpert (or no longer expert) supervisor can fall into equally dangerous traps if he tries too hard to compensate for his inadequacies. One of the most common dodges of the one-upped supervisor is the counterexpertise play: "Well, I don't know anything about the Khmers; I'll be the first to acknowledge it; but I remember a situation very like this Southeast Asia thing we are discussing which took place some time back when I was in Central America, and I can tell you. ..."

The old timing game, of course, is played by both sides in this contest of generations. How often has the drafter of a paper come rushing into a senior's office, saying, breathlessly, "Hope you can read this right away, sir. I spent all weekend on it and it's got to go to the DD this afternoon. Incidentally, the girls have started typing, so I hope you won't have too many suggestions." Of course, there have been a few times when a supervisor has stopped a staff man in the hall, saying, "By the way, I had lunch with the DD and he asked about that paper you gave me to look at. I thought I had better give it to him right away. Sorry I didn't have time to consult with you about it, particularly as I rewrote the last section and put it at the beginning."

Well, we're not all perfect, and this sort of thing goes on partly because in many cases things would not get done if it didn't. The point here seems to be that the better a man the expert is and the better a man the supervisor is, the less the need for stratagems. So, if you're an expert, get a good supervisor, and if you're a supervisor. ...

There are, of course, a good many pitfalls that specialists and non-specialists together can get into. One of the worst, both from the point of view of the people involved and of the whole Intelligence Community, is a syndrome best represented by the famed "numbers game". The problem usually arises when there is a strongly felt need on the part of the top users of intelligence for a degree of precision which the evidence, or, indeed, often the subject, does not permit. When the top policy makers ask, for example, "How many Russians are there in Cuba anyway? Just give us your best guess." The people down the line ought to be very cautious, we all know now, about giving them a figure at all unless there is a certain minimum evidentiary basis for it. The consequence, of course, can be finding ourselves unable to change figures even when our intelligence improves, because of the difficulty of explaining how we got the original figures on the books anyway. All this adds up to one of the most important rules for the intelligence officer: Don't fool yourself into thinking that if higher authority demands it, it makes sense to put out something that is basically unsound.

The intelligence officer's working life is not spent only at his desk or in consultation with his supervisor. There is the group: the meeting, the committee, the task force, the discussion, the debriefing—all standard situations in the intelligence culture. These intelligence group's experiences might not seem to some to be as dramatic as what we are told goes on at the Esalen Institute in California where people grope, in the company of others, for self-understanding, but they can be pretty real and earnest. They probably produce as much self-realization and as much bloodshed as similar competitive situations anywhere. On any good workday one will find as wide a variety of successful personal styles on display in intelligence groups, as in a Madison Avenue idea session, in a back boardroom, or an academic committee.

Every experienced participant in group intelligence knows the country boy who talks of the inner mysteries of Soviet space technology with just enough of a southern drawl to add a human touch. There is the blustering Devil's advocate who specializes in outlandish and unanswerable propositions. There is the man with a cause who specializes in stripping the flesh off the proponents of a rival school of analysis. There is the specialist in the scathing personal attack at the right moment. (My favorite, and one done in good humor, is an instance where criticism of a sentence in a draft paper was conceded by the author to have been "ambivalent." "Sir," said the critic, "You do yourself too much credit. An ambivalent sentence has two meanings. Yours has none at all.")

Along with the bad guys, and the bores, the sycophants, and the fools intelligence officers may be carefully screened, but no foolproof battery of tests has yet been devised—there are, naturally a fair proportion of good guys of all sorts. Here, as elsewhere, the observer of the intelligence culture must conclude that the fact that intelligence people are people is all to the good, as well as being unavoidable. Furthermore, it does not obscure or change the fact that, whatever the style, the ability to produce sound intelligence is the payoff in the end.

There is still another situation in which intelligence officers interact and which gives rise to its share of specialized behavior patterns. I refer to the joys of coordination, particularly of that highest form of agony known as interagency coordination. Getting things done within an agency, as amply suggested above, is complex enough, but in an interagency situation, where the boss can't resolve the disputes, a very specialized form of interaction takes place. How it all works, I shan't pretend that I understand, though there are a few clues. When the Navy representative says, "Can't you please mention submarines in the section?" his colleagues are inclined to go along if it won't mess up the paper too much and if he can be expected to be agreeable when their turn comes. Perhaps the most time-honored and symbolic device of the interagency coordination process is the convention of bestowing "The Order of the Lion" on a representative who has done his duty and manfully presented his superior's case to an unreceptive audience. (The idea is that he can go back home and tell the boss that he fought like a lion but that the other agencies wouldn't have it.)

Nowhere else is the art of the tradeoff so highly developed. Nowhere else is such skill applied to the artful suggestion of a different form of words to say what is already in the text in order to save the face of a colleague who can neither withdraw nor make his proposal specific. The worst burden for coordinators is the colleague who insists that he, or his boss, doesn't like something but doesn't know why or what he wants to do about it. The greatest problem, of course, is the intervention of departmental interest, or policy commitment, into the discussion of an intelligence judgment. Most representatives realize that this is a high crime—or at least that it stultifies the process—but all tend to be sympathetic with the colleague who they know has to go back to a boss who doesn't know or care about the distinction between intelligence and policy. The miracle is that interagency coordination of intelligence works as well as it does, that the people who do it get along, and that the end product is almost always sound intelligence.

What is there to conclude from all this? That we are people, like other people, and that our personalities, our instinctive drives, and our subconscious minds get deeply involved in the process of "knowing the truth"? I believe so, and I believe it is essential that we acknowledge and take account of this while doing our best to create as much as possible of that marvelous stuff, objective intelligence, which is what Allen Dulles probably had in mind when he selected that quote from the Bible.

Bibliography

1 We do not propose to set down all the "laws of intelligence," but only those commonly cited or applied in the production of intelligence. Kent's Law, for instance of any coup d'état I have heard of isn't going to happen"—is a profound truth but not within the scope of this paper.

2 *Studies* Vol. 13, No. 4, pp. 89-90.

DO STYLIN'

Ed's Note: The Directorate of Operations, later known as the National Clandestine Service, does not spend anywhere near the same amount of time as the DI in agonizing over the search for *le mot juste*. This is not to say that competent communications skills are not prized by case officers and their colleagues. Richard T. Puderbaugh made this case in "Elegant Writing in the Clandestine Services: In which it appears things aren't getting any better" in a *Studies in Intelligence* article. Kudos to the Center for the Study of Intelligence for declassifying this gem.

// ⊕ //

How I came to be designated CWH/WW (Chief Word Watcher, Western Hemisphere) was that a certain Senior Officer called me into his office the other day and showed me a paper from one of the stations, which spoke of giving an operation "short shift."* My God, he said, who ever heard of a short shift? I knew what he meant, so I didn't make the mistake of mentioning Volkswagens, 1970 petticoats or the Redskins. The Senior Officer went on with his denunciation, and ended up by asking me "Don't they know what 'shrift' means?"

It is a good question. How many people do know? It is one of those terms everybody knows about and thinks he can define, and one which should really lead people inexorably to the dictionary. But it doesn't, not even those people who know how to spell it. I didn't say these things to the Senior Officer, because he is more senior than I am, and has a quick temper.

Anyway, in that conversation, the Senior Officer appointed me Official Word Watcher for the Division, by I don't know what authority, and charged me with the following duties:

To collect from all CS communications outstanding examples of elegant writing, and to report upon my research at opportune times so that our writers may be edified and instructed thereby.

As soon as my appointment became known, I had a great deal of help from other headquarters personnel, but I will acknowledge that help specifically only if the danger of lynching becomes clear, and I need help (or company).

Here, then, is my first report. I should like to begin it by listing some of the most elegant words we have in our correspondence, words which I urge one and all to use at every opportunity. I should like to see the day when not a single page of our prose escapes the use of at least one of these words. I especially urge our writers to try new uses for all these words, and not be bound by such things as tense, gender, number or mode. *Caveat*, for example, is in the Latin imperative mode, but that is much too restrictive, and we have quite properly used this word as a noun for some time now. Imagine my delight when I observed recently the first attempt that I know of to use it, as is, in the present indicative. When you consider that we have long since expanded its original sense of "warning" to include the sense of "conditions" or "provisos," you can understand why the word is so important to us. I can right here remark that I should caveat some of the remarks I am about to make in this essay, and you will not have the slightest idea what I mean, but it sounds distinguished and important, and that is what matters.

Here is the list:
- caveat
- rationale
- thrust

- interface (used as a noun and a verb)
- dichotomy
- lacuna*
- forthcoming (in the sense of "candid")
- profile (can be either high or low)
- silhouette (can be either high or low)
- options
- life-style
- posture
- rapport

Rapport is an especially fine word, but so far we have used it only as a noun. Perhaps we should offer a prize to the officer who first devises a successful sentence using rapport as a verb, although we may have been beaten to the punch on this one by the folk-rock expression "to rap." Even employing "rapport" as a noun, nevertheless, we can do great things. Note the following excerpt from a field report:

"We hope it does not reach the extreme where the agent fails to establish a working rapport, or worse, and thus destroys …"

The mind boggles at the thought of anything being worse than a working rapport, and yet here is an officer who does *not* want the agent to *fail* to establish exactly that. Like the character in the play who suddenly discovered that he had been speaking prose all his life, this writer is probably unaware that he has constructed a litotes there. A litotes affirms something by denying the contrary, as in "he is not without charm." The device can also be stretched to refute something by negating the denial of the contrary, as in "he denied that he was not unwilling to go," … and so on, into total opacity. It is one way to make a reader really study your prose. Still with me?

Try this one:

"Subject: Refutal of rumors regarding a coup."

To take words from other languages or disciplines, and use them in new and clever ways to confound the pedestrian mind, is a noble thing, but how much more magnificent it is to take a legitimate word from our own language and by the change of one phoneme devise a new word, which nobody ever heard of before, but whose meaning everybody will immediately perceive! The roots of this particular treasure seem to be in the words *refuse* and *refute*, but I noted that the inventor did not arrange a reciprocal loan of suffixes and speak of such things as "Hanoi's *refusation* to make peace." There is something not quite right about that one. Sort of low class, perhaps. It is possible, of course, that the word rebut was bobbing around in the crucible which produced *refutal*, but in that direction lies paranoia, and we will venture no farther.

It seems to me that *refutal* deserves at least as high a place in our lexicon as *normalcy*, which, as you may know, was invented by Warren G. Harding, who didn't realize he was inventing anything. He would have made a good operations officer. Indeed, I think that the authenticity of these inventions has to be based to a great extent upon the fact that when they are first uttered their inventors are unconscious of bringing something new into the world.

I don't know whether the innocence of the inventors has any bearing on the acceptability of words to modern dictionaries. I doubt it. Modern dictionaries will accept anything anybody says, because if somebody says something it becomes usage, and usage is king! There is one grumpy headquarters officer who dislikes this modern trend, and says that the Oxford of 1912 is the only authoritative dictionary of the English language. He is a troublemaker, who will one day be dealt with by Division Authorities. He is the one who brought to me the following:

"Subject: Easement of the Threat of a Coup."

I had to point out to him that Webster's New World Dictionary says there *is* such a meaning to easement, in addition to the legal use pertaining to land titles, so that settles that. He also has to accept the fact, for instance, that chaise longue has now become *chaise lounge* in this country, by authority of Sears, Roebuck and Company, and that *lingerie* means ladies' drawers and shifts and things of that nature, and if he and the French don't like it then they can damn well lump it.

What should we do about the shall/will problem? My own inclination is to let it lie, because the shall/will rule was an artificial thing, anyway, set up in a very elegant epoch of the English language, to tone up the speech of His Majesty's subjects. It is a difficult thing to master, and I think we are doing well enough without it, although you have to admit that nothing dresses up a sentence quite so much as an unexpected "shall" where a "will" really belongs. That is to say that we should pay no attention to the rule, but should just put in a shall at any time a sentence needs to be toned up a bit.

Another problem which I'm inclined to de-emphasize is the one which the *New Yorker* calls "The Omnipotent Whom." There is no doubt about it, whom sounds much more literate and polished than plain old everyday who, but I think we have this factor under good control. In fact, I have ceased collecting samples, after nearly filling a notebook, because everyone is doing so well. I shall cite just two fairly typical examples:

> "(individual), whom we note is currently in Paris ..."
>
> "Forward the document to whomever may have an interest in the matter."

If there is anything that dresses up our prose even more than the shall/will or who/whom pilasters, it is the mixed metaphor. If your metaphor gives a clear picture, you should be ashamed of yourself. We don't do as well as we should on metaphors, in fact, and we must work on them a bit harder. We have much to learn from the State Department in this respect, as witness the following sample from State traffic:

> "If the government of Graustark does not box itself in by wrapping the national flag around the training area ..."

Try to construct a mental picture from the Ozymandian blueprint, and despair! The same State Department expert also spoke of "a certain rustling of sabers," which shows that he is made of championship material. I would quarrel mildly in one sense, however. If the sabers are, in truth, made of something that rustles, he should correct and extend his borrowing from Poe, and make the rustling uncertain, as well as sad, and perhaps silken. Unless, of course, the writer meant to imply that there was a kind of military Bad Bart who was going around stealing great numbers of sabers from the corrals of nice folks in white hats.

But a fig for the State Department! We have our own experts, and I defy any other agency to produce anything to equal the following:

> "The result of the medical checkup was that the agent has diabetes."
>
> "His bank allotee is forwarded under separate cover."
>
> "The negative reaction to this device was its (attaboy!) lack of sufficient range. It was tested singularly and in pairs."
>
> "He is not temperamentally geared to write in subtilities, but does produce good hardhitting yellow journalism in the style of a poor man's Westbrook Pegler."

The last sentence may be one of the best of the decade. I don't say that because of his reference to "hardhitting" journalism, either, even though that term does limn a picture of an energetic, up-and-at-'em CIA officer playing Wagnerian themes on the mighty Wurlitzer he has constructed from his local (sob) *stable of assets*. It's good, but you can't give very high marks for it, because when you come right down to it, our operations have never to my knowledge produced a single paragraph that *wasn't* hardhitting. Where that sentence achieves greatness is in calling attention to one of the characteristics of the late columnist which has been too long overlooked — that is, the fact that only the rich could afford the real Westbrook Pegler.

But there is more. If one lifts the phrase "temperamentally geared" out of the stream and contemplates it carefully, one cannot help but be impressed with the subtility of the thing. I know a number of people in this agency who I think are temperamentally geared. I steer clear of them. They can't do you any good.

> "In view of the serious flap potential, which, if discovered by the host government, could have lead to a worsening of relations ..."

We need not dwell upon the construction which hypothesizes the damage that might be done if the government discovers the flap potential of an operation. We all know that, surely. Who among us would ever want a host government to find out how risky an operation he was mounting? We must always keep our host government reassured that our clandestine operations in their countries have also no flap potential at all. But let us press on to the rest of that sentence, whose enigmatic wording led my mind into an almost psychedelic whirl, with images of "some lead is red, and some reds are led," and when the machinery finally clanked to a halt, here is what came out of the printer:

Wherever your writing may lead, Sir,
You may rest assured I shall read, Sir;
But if, when I've read,
You insist I've been lead,
Then I surely shall sea read, indeed, Sir.

You can have that, if you want it.
    Perhaps there is something about lead that attracts the many Freudian associations with bullets or poison or pollution. It would not be the first time our prose implied more than it said. Notice the gothic scene evoked by the following:

> "... we will continue to keep this asset tabled, and will call on him for spot reporting when necessary."

If all our Operations Officers were as skilled at writing as this man, the Green Beret case would never have hit the headlines. There is no "terminated with extreme prejudice" blooper here to provoke the news media into soaring flights of fancy. No, the untutored mind would receive that sentence as meaning that the matter was being held in abeyance, as in the parliamentary term "to table a motion," whereas those of us in the know immediately perceive that this officer is describing a bit of standard tradecraft, whereby we strap a man to a deal table and belabor him with interfaces and rapports and dichotomies until he by God comes up with a spot report.

> "So successful was Fulano's re-immergence as a crusading journalist that ..."

A number of our stations have in the past produced or supported underground newspapers, but this must be the first one of record whose clandestine journalism was done under water. Eat your heart out, MI-6!

> "Fulano appears to be in excellent financial straits."
>
> "Subject and his wife, Josephine, nee unknown ..."
>
> "He did it in a fit of peak."*
>
> "He easily looses his head."
>
> "He attempted to illicit the information."
>
> "The rightist candidate, who won a plurality of votes.
>
> "The agent demonstrated an excellent operational posture."*
>
> ... like operating in a vacuum tube."
>
> "The national liveration movement ...'
>
> "Incendiary fires will be set."
>
> "Several methods of modus operandi are being contemplated."

The author of that last sentence could have added immeasurably to its charm by pointing out that incendiary fires can be put out with wet water; but he did at least clarify things a bit the following week by explaining "By large incendiary fires, the agent may be referring to one of the petroleum storage areas ..."

One of the prize words in my collection is the invention of a State Department officer, whom we really ought to try to identify and recruit. The word is fragile and beautiful, and it is with some hesitation that I offer it up on our rather brutal altar, for I fear that we will over-use it and cause it to wilt and fade before its time. I have no right to keep it, however, and present it herewith with a fervent exhortation to one and all to use it tenderly so that it will last for at least six months to a year. Here it is:

dichotomization

If that doesn't bring a lump to your throat, nothing will. There is more, but I cannot go on. I trust you will all keep your passive voice active. It must never be allowed to be wondered why our communications are not being written with more thrust and rationale. Go forth and write, and may the Lord have rapport upon you.

Footnotes

*Author's Note: In this essay, examples of elegant writing have been taken from official CS communications. The names of originating stations and officers, as well as cryptonyms and other indicators, have been changed to protect the guilty. (*Ed's note:* CS: Clandestine Service)

* Plural is *lacunae*. This is really a keen word, which has only recently appeared. Used judiciously, it should be OK at least through 1973.

* Fit of peak is known to the medical profession as "Pike's Syndrome." In Asia, it is called "Norky's Complaint."

* The OK operational posture for 1970-72, in case you didn't know, is *forward-leaning*. We have in the past been through postures of defense, agonizing re-appraisal, benevolent neutrality and the like, but then came that luminous moment when an unknown genius suggested that we should all be forward-leaning. Thousands of our patriotic, conscientious Headquarters staff members were thereupon transformed into human gnomons,

who can be observed every morning shortly before 8:30, inclined dutifully in the direction of Langley, and at about 5:00 p.m. pointed just as dutifully toward home.

Ed's Note: Puderbaugh's research into DO writing paid off a second time, when he wrote "Elegant Writing: Report Number Two: the pen is sometimes flightier than the words" for Studies in Intelligence. Herewith are the additional fruits of his work:

If you missed my first report,* I should explain to you that I have been designed Chief Word Watcher, Western Hemisphere Division, and have been instructed to submit reports from time to time on outstanding examples of elegant writing in what is best known as the Clandestine Service. It has been some months since my first report, and I must say that I have been impressed by the response. Elegant writing has definitely begun to attract the attention of our officers.

There are some areas which still need improvement, nevertheless. Too many of our writers are still utilizing the word "use" where they could just as well use "utilize" and get the same meaning out of it. The mitigate/militate ratio is merely holding its own, when in fact we ought to be expanding our use of "mitigate against." As to the flout/flaunt ratio, we may even be losing ground, and I urge you all to be especially watchful for instances of contempt for the law so that we can be sure that it gets flaunted rather than flouted.

There is also one point which I failed to make in my first report, because quite frankly I didn't think we were having any trouble with it, but I now find that that is not the case. The problem is in the modern and forceful use of the words *target, aim, fault,* and *blame*. It is old fashioned to aim at a target. One targets at an aim these days. The same can be said for blaming people for being at fault. Today we fault them for being to blame. This is a process of shaping meanings which delights us veteran word watchers, and I can even see possibilities in these words for an entire reversal of meaning, as happened with our old friend sanction. Think of the linguistic genius it required to give one word two diametrically opposed meanings! "The U.N. today sanctioned sanctions against Israel." It is an aim we should target at.

Here are a few samples of elegant writing, selected at random from my collection of the past six months:

> "The actions must be completed in as quickly a time as possible."
>
> "Transmitted hereto for your retention and information…"
>
> "We regret that reference cable was ambivalent and apparently misleading."
>
> "They described him as a friendly type who loves entertaining people."
>
> "He has been out visiting the grass roots."

As you read, it will become evident to you that our best work during this period has been in our descriptions of people and the things they do. One of the most impressive of these is the following: "Although sleeping at the time of the officer's contact, the American Consul talked to Mr. Doe on 25 September, and was lucid and alert." You can't tell whether that is a dangling participle or a *non sequitur,* and therein lies its charm.

> "The reference, made in a letter, by Doe's wife to Doe having gotten himself involved in espionage, though, might be indicative of something, albeit enigmatic."
>
> "He believes the risk will be minimal* if students and instructors utilize reasonable jurisprudence in the course of the exercise."
>
> "He incurred the intense displeasure of the war ministry and general officers close to the president recently by pubically advocating abolition of the congressional authority."

I showed that last one to my friend, the Senior Officer, who pronounced it a typographical error and therefore not really deserving of high marks. I would agree if it were only the absence of the "l" between the "b" and the "i", but the addition of the "al" as the penultimate syllable can hardly be a typographical error. The author of that sentence therefore gets top grades from me for his effort, especially since he had the great good sense to avoid any actual description of the gestures a man makes when he pubically advocates something.

> "This announcement by the two officials should put an end to specific rumors of one firing the other, or vice versa."
>
> "At that time they were in the first stages of a broken marriage."
>
> "Even the carrot and stick approach of offering a higher income did not produce results."
>
> "The old man, although infirm, obviously is not on his dying bed."

The following three quotations demonstrate what I have come to call the Puderbaugh Principle of Traumatic Terseness. We all know what a great impact one can achieve by making portentous statements in few words. "Lafayette, we are here." "I cannot spare this general. He fights." Now observe how much greater an impact can be achieved when the short statement describes the totally unexpected—not to say unbelievable:

> "Doe and his wife had a daughter of four. When he last saw her she was pregnant."
>
> "Fulano's wife is in her late twenties and their daughter, Mary, is aged about four. The latter is rather pale and sickly. She doesn't like Graustark very much. She smokes."
>
> "Mengano was one of seven children, and was raised without a father who was killed by a log in a forest."

Given the rather consistent distortion of our work by the news media, the public might be pardoned for supposing that people in our profession live in a James Bond kind of world. If the truth were to be told (and it can certainly be deduced from the foregoing demonstrations of Puderbaugh's Principle) ours is much more of a Tolkien world than a Bond world. The people we deal with are surrounded by dangers Bond never dreamed of, and that may explain why they feel impelled to begin enjoying life, and reproducing it, at a very early age.

While we are on the subject of descriptions of persons and their doings, I must announce with some sadness that a writer from another agency has won this year's Grand Prize for Baroque Bloviation. CIA has done some fine things, but nothing to compare with the following analysis which a Defense Department officer wrote about the wife of a government official in his country of assignment:

> "She has a presentable personality with a modern posture, who is well versed in world affairs, where by modern standards she is considered to be a whole person."

Another non-CIA writer has been granted an honorable mention for excellence in Freudian Implications. He is a senior Foreign Service Officer at one of our embassies, who informed his Washington office:

> "The editor of a respected weekly called on me today to discuss the current political situation which he predicted would come to an end very soon."

It must be the golden dream, the cherished Nirvana, of our harried friends in the State Department—that moment when a political situation comes to an end.*

In no other instance did I find our writers to have been vested by those of other agencies, although I do have an item of special interest from USAID which I shall present to you later in this report. Our writers are especially good in those constructions which separate vital sentence parts from one another and place high-class words between them, selected and arranged so as to give the reader many minutes of enchantment as he searches for the meaning. The first of these sentences also evokes folk-feelings of the ancient past, echoing the syntax of the Germanic Mother Tongue.

> "He helped his daughter, with whom he is quite close, out financially."
>
> "We feel that the university, while still an important target, is less so that it once was. Even if it were, the situation on campus makes the operation impossible."

The beauty of that last quotation at first seemed to me to lie in its antecedent anarchy. Upon closer examination I discovered that the anarchy is much more pervasive than a mere indiscipline of pronouns and their antecedents. Here it is entire thoughts which are launched from their pads and enter orbit without ever achieving rendezvous with sister components.

Closely related to the foregoing examples of skillful disarticulation of sentence parts is the practice of redundancy. It is not difficult to be redundant, of course, and no special merit attaches to the mere repetition of a thought twice in several dozen words, but when you can express the same idea three times in five words you are in a class by yourself:

> "That would make his estimated ETA on or about 5 July."

For technically excellence in tautology, that sentence is the best of the season, but for a symmetry which closely approaches poetry I think we would have to give the prize to this one:

> "If Doe were arrested as soon as feasibly possible..."

There are some sentences which mirror a truly and innately elegant soul—a writer who not only puts down elegant sentences, but whose thoughts are elegantly arranged. Here is a sentence which comes from the mind of just such an aristocrat, a writer who is modern enough to have no compunction about ending a sentence with a preposition, but who at the same time steadfastly avoids any ellipsis of relative pronouns:

> "In order to return, he had to be guaranteed work and a house which to move into."

I shall now list a number of items which do not fall into any special Wordwatcher classification, but which deserve our respectful attention all the same:

> "The SDNT, the largest and only exile group in Graustark…"
>
> "He was determined not to defend red tape for its own sake."
>
> "Misnomering of ammunition is illegal."
>
> "We apologize for the readability of the copies."*
>
> "Parallelly, we plan to start work on another project."
>
> "We opted not to reopen the question to avoid the risk of needlessly beating a dead horse."**
>
> "That would be opening the magic Pandora's box."
>
> "We would be foolhearty if we were to dismiss it lightly."
>
> "They threw Molotov cocktails against five downtown stores during daylight hours in lightening demonstrations."

A word is in order here about *lightening demonstrations*. I have had many discussions about this with associates in Headquarters who had never been to the field, and who think the reference is really to *lightning demonstrations*. It is surprising that this kind of objection can come from people who live in Washington, D.C., for they have witnessed the real thing right in their own city. Briefly, any demonstration which reduces a downtown store's inventory by several tons, or sets fire to its premises, can without hesitation be classed as a *lightening demonstration*. Demonstrations which include the use of Molotov cocktails are, by definition, *lightening* ones.

I was especially pleased during this period to see that one writer had extended the use of the word *majority* beyond anything our people had ever dared before. There had been a serious flood in his area of assignment, and in due course he reported that "the majority of the water had receded," and thereby implied that there was a minority of the water still around. From sad experience, however, I had learned not to trust such statements about the majority of, say, the money, or the weather, or the pollution, because I have found that many of our writers don't really know the definition of *majority*, and may in fact be talking about a plurality of these things. So I recommend great care with this usage.

In conclusion I want to report to you about a writer who works for USAID, who recently came to my attention. I know we must not proselyte, but if there is any way to get this man to transfer to our agency we should try our best to do it. He is clearly of managerial stature. He writes:

> "We must steer a careful course between doing nothing about future plans and doing the irrelevant."

That statement comes close to the beauty of Ring Lardner's masterpiece, "Although he was not a good outfield, he was not a good hitter, either." It is a question of keeping one part of a sentence from ever knowing what the other part is doing, and it is this kind of perfection toward which we must continue to strive. Few of us can hope to attain such high levels of elegance, but we must not let the seeming unattainability of the goal keep us from doing our best at all times. You can rest assured that any activity you engage in to equal or better the foregoing examples of elegant writing will be sanctioned by the highest authority."

Footnotes
- Studies in Intelligence, XVv1.
- "Minimal" is a very OK word this year.

- The moment when a political situation reaches its zenith, on the other hand, has never been better described than by a State cable from North Africa in the mid-50's which may antedate Mr. Puderbaugh's research: "The seething cauldron is approaching the crossroad, and it is beyond the power of the French to get it back on the tracks." One sighs that these cables had no visual aids. [Editor.]

- An apology which might well be made for much of our official correspondence.

- Analogies have a way of losing their relevance as years pass. The writer of this sentence was wise enough to perceive that dead horses are not what they used to be. One must be careful to distinguish between those dead horses which it is bootless to beat, and those which can be turned into a profitable enterprise only by the application of the bastinado.

NOTES FROM THE CIA'S IN-BOX

Ed's note: In addition to the thousands of conventional letters, e-mails, phone calls, and other communications the CIA's Office of Public Affairs reviews, asking for information, autographed photos of the DCI, or just to express the thanks of a grateful nation, come numerous oddities. Most are well-meaning, some are ravings, and others are merely hilarious. Our thanks to CIA's Center for the Study of Intelligence for declassifying an early Studies in Intelligence article by David R. McLean on "Cranks, Nuts, and Screwballs", from which we've drawn these excerpts.

// ⊕ //

"I have always had adequate sex that no one appreciated. I need a better grade of iron to eat, and so do the astronauts." *(Excerpt from a July 1964 letter to the Director of Central Intelligence.)*

// ⊕ //

"A defenseless woman having husband trouble sincerely requests your help." *(June 1964 letter to the DCI, enclosing picture of a convertible and address of a suburban motel.)*

// ⊕ //

"O.K.! Keep me off the payroll. I'll try and sell my abilities to the Soviet Union." *(1965 postcard peevishly addressed to the U.S. Lower Intelligence Agency.)*

// ⊕ //

"Please be informed, old pal, I have entered my name with the 87th Congress as a candidate for the Presidency of the United States in the next elections. If I make it, I am going to reinstate you in CIA." *(1962 letter to Allen W. Dulles.)*

// ⊕ //

"You can tell John A. McCone to go to hell if you think I'm going to be treated this way after all I've done for you people." *(Early morning telephone call from "Agent 44" on his release from the drunk cell of a Washington police precinct.)*

// ⊕ //

"ORNISCOPYTHEOBI BLIOPSYCHOCRYSI ARROSCIO-AEROGEN ETHLIOMETEOR OAU STRAHIEROANTHRO VICHTHYOPYROSI DEROCH PNOMYOALE ..." *(Excerpt from a 1963 telegram to CIA.)*

// ⊕ //

Something about a secret intelligence agency attracts an endless stream of letters, cards, telegrams, phone calls, and personal visits from deranged, possibly dangerous, or merely daffy citizens who want to horn in on the cloak-and-dagger act. Mixed into the CIA morning mail, these unsolicited testimonials to the Agency's drawing power create some delicate screening problems, waste a lot of time, and justify elaborate security precautions to protect its top officials.

The Agency's Office of Security keeps a watch list of persons or organizations who have tried to visit, write, or phone its officials and who have been, at a minimum, a source of annoyance. Every suspected crank contact is checked against this list. The signatures include "The Green Russian" in Charlotte, N.C., and "Your Aunt Minnie" in San Francisco. Nearly all crank letters are domestic, but alongside addresses in Pewee Valley, Ky., and Big Bear City, Cal., are foreign listings from Quito to Warsaw and from Edinburgh to Australia.

Steadies and One-Timers

The flow of oddball letters and phone calls increases perceptibly when CIA is in the news. Less than 48 hours after President Johnson announced he would nominate Admiral Raborn to be the DCI, a Detroit man had sent the Director-designate 8,000 words of complaint about the high cost of prescription medicines and a New Yorker had asked his help in controlling a whistling brain. The file of letters to him was mounting even before his appointment had been confirmed. On 17 April a Massachusetts man sent him some well-intentioned advice. "Dear Admiral," he wrote, "as you may be aware, L.B.J. ain't got much Brains or he wouldn't be President. I dealt with his type for 37 years. The best way to get along with him is humor him."

But a faithful nucleus of loyal intelligence fans always contributes about 25 percent of the total. Probably most of the cranks are as harmless as the childish codes they sometimes use. The trouble is, they're unpredictable. A few might have complaints worth hearing; others might pose a real threat to an unsuspecting officer who received them.

Nut-and-dolt visits to headquarters offices have practically disappeared since CIA moved out to Langley; an occasional walk-in still calls at its personnel office downtown. Its overt or semi-overt domestic offices, which are more approachable, have now compiled an impressive record of coping with off-beat visitors.

Clairvoyance and Contrivances

A fairly common complaint of the walk-ins is getting messages from the Communists by thought-transference or through the fillings in their teeth. One disturbed gentleman from Buffalo claimed the Communists had kidnapped him, cut open his head, removed his brains, and substituted a radio. After warning his interviewer to say nothing the opposition should not hear, he asked CIA to remove the radio and replace the brains. For sheer imagination in fielding such a complaint, the prize probably goes to the CIA man who assured a woman she might indeed be getting radio messages by static electricity. Reminding her of the chains that drag under gasoline trucks, he linked a series of paper clips, hooked one end in her skirt, let the other end trail on the floor, and sent her happily on her way with the static safely grounded.

Then there was the man who came in to volunteer as a spy in the Czechoslovakian uranium mines. He confided that he had been stalling because he feared the radiation might make him sterile. Now, however, he had solved this problem: he planned to carry along a carton of Chesterfields and wrap the tinfoil around his private parts. The Agency secretary who transcribed a memorandum on his visit never could understand why he insisted on Chesterfields.

Some fairly far-out ideas have been seriously proposed by sensible citizens. One responsible businessman developed a mechanical chess-playing machine which countered any move according to prepunched IBM cards. He proposed to take his machine to Moscow, consolidate his position there, and then suggest that the machine could be used as a training aid for any move-and-countermove situation, such as military tactics. Instead of chessmen he would use symbols for tanks, infantry, hills, forests, planes, and fields of fire. Since he knew nothing about military tactics, the Soviet general staff would have to tell him the prescribed response to every move. As soon as he had all the responses punched on IBM cards he would deliver duplicates to the American Embassy. Then if we ever faced the USSR in battle we could always run the IBM cards and tell what the Soviets would do next.

The most intriguing case investigated by a domestic office involved a school superintendent of unassailable reliability who dabbled in hypnotism as a hobby and reported that he could induce clairvoyance in his subject, an engineering student. In 1957, while in a hypnotic trance, the subject described in minute technical detail a Soviet ballistic missile of a type unknown in the United States but consistent with expert private assessments of Soviet capabilities. The research chief of a respected American aircraft plant was present at the demonstration, framed many questions, and made a tape recording of the answers. The subject used technical and scientific terminology which neither he nor the hypnotist could be expected to know. Washington experts who studied the tape found "just enough substantive data to stimulate the imagination" but decided that clairvoyance would be "a very risky approach to the collection of Soviet guided missile data." The mystery remains unsolved.

Other Field Office Walk-ins

Some unlikely sources have produced usable information. In 1959 a soldier of fortune fresh from Cuba wearing yellow canvas shoes, red denim slacks, and a gaudy sport shirt contacted a domestic office. His debriefing was worthwhile but abbreviated by his arrest for having a bag of dynamite in his hotel room. In October 1964 a Miami man brought to CIA a box which he had bought sight-unseen at an auction of shipments abandoned in U.S. customs. The box contained more than 2,000 negatives of Cuban propaganda. And on 8 July 1960, an admitted swindler and diamond smuggler volunteered the information that five Soviet missile experts had just travelled to Cuba by way of Mexico. This report was taken with a grain of salt at the time.

One probable James Bond fan seems obsessed with finding unusual ways of eliminating the opposition. Besides the usual poisons and trick guns, he has suggested a lethally exploding cigar disguised with a band reading "It's a boy!" He has also offered to dispose of bodies for us in his home meat grinder. An attractive divorcee leads a sober life in this country as an airline secretary but regularly flies to another country and cuts loose there among the political leaders. For all her Mata Hari complex she has brought useful information.

Ever since 1948, a Slovak economist has been trying to peddle information he claims to obtain through a private underground net. He is presentable and persuasive and has impressed countless high officials, including a senator who brought him to lunch with the upper echelons of CIA. Fortunately these official contacts quickly lead back to a burn notice identifying him as a fabricator. As late as 1963, however, he was still trying with some success to interest leading American industries in technical data from anti-Communist researchers behind the Iron Curtain. Having abandoned the atomic cannon he offered the government, he was tempting industry with everything from synthetic fibers to jet engine designs, high-temperature ceramics, and flexible concrete. Meanwhile he had hired a lawyer and sued a Washington shoe store for $25,000 because his shoes were too tight; in the brief he filed with the court he claimed that as a spy he needed to run fast.

Letters to Langley

By far the greatest number of crank contacts are by mail. In the first eight months of Fiscal Year 1965, 1,143 letters addressed simply to CIA were identified as from cranks. This does not count those addressed otherwise—to the DCI by name or to specific field offices.

Neither does it include some unsolicited letters which may be helpful, pathetic, or merely misguided but are not from cranks. The following examples are all from March 1965: An ex-Marine sent a possibly practical suggestion for guerrilla warfare. A 17-year-old Thai girl asked how to get training in police investigation. A German student asked for help in locating his father, who had been captured by the Soviets in World War II. A 14-year-old boy asked if there were really such organizations as SMERSH and U.N.C.L.E. All such writers receive courteous replies.

But in the same month there arrived elaborate greetings to the DCI from a Maryland woman who thinks she is Catherine III, Empress of all the Russias, and who had previously sent a 5,000-word report on how she ensured the successful invasion of Europe by entertaining Hitler privately for 12 hours on D-Day. Also in March 1965 came the advice that "now is the time—at last—to train 100 of the top CIA men to penetrate every possible beauty parlor and Chinese restaurant ... the results will amaze and constantly astound your organization." On 13 March a New York correspondent informed us that Rudolph Hess, from his cell in Spandau, was controlling ten leading Southern segregationists by long-distance hypnotism. And on 25 March a woman wrote to the Director from Massachusetts: "As near as I can make out there normally is a grey cloud at the base of the psyche. When the cloud backs up you go out of focus. But after taking Alka Seltzer and sodium bicarbonate I can sing Hokus Pokus you're in focus."

A 1964 letter was addressed to "Snuffy McDuffy, Top Floor, Closed Door, CIA, Washington, D.C." Perceptive mail clerks sent it to the Director's office, where it was found to contain a fairly reasonable suggestion for propaganda. The letter ended: "P.S. If you don't take appropriate action I'll write to the President and tell him you're chicken."

The Fox

Probably the most imaginative and persistent correspondent is a gaunt long-faced man with sunken eyes and prominent ears who first wrote to CIA on 27 January 1952 asking for a high-powered rifle with telescopic sights and terrain maps of Siberia, Manchuria, and Korea. Since then he has sent thousands of letters, postcards, and telegrams and used more than 50 aliases ranging from "Alexis Alexandrovich" to "Old Woody, The Fox." Usually he signs his true name followed by "U.S. Code 143," CIA's government tie-line code. Here we shall call him Old Woody.

Even though his handwriting and literary style are well known around the DCI's office, age cannot wither nor custom stale Old Woody's infinite variety. One letter told the Director: "I have allotted you a maximum life span of 94 years, not to exceed the year 1987." Another complained that "someone has wired my head for sight and sound." A third urged the Director to "tell Hoffa to require seat belts in all trucks." A fourth began: "Allen, I regret to inform you Kennedy won the election fair and square." Then came a telegram (collect) from Florida: "REQUEST FEDERAL TROOPS, MARTIAL LAW. MIAMI SITUATION OUT OF CONTROL."

Old Woody travels widely, usually first class. He has written from Cuba, Puerto Rico, Nassau, Honolulu, and Hong Kong, as well as from most major cities in the United States. On domestic airlines and in American hotels he has often registered as "A.W. Dulles, Jr." and mailed cancelled tickets and receipted bills to CIA. He likes luxury hotels; his suite at a Washington hotel in 1960 was billed at $52 a day. On many of his trips he listed CIA's street address as his residence and the DCI as his next-of-kin, often reinforcing the latter claim by taking out $62,500 in flight insurance with the Director as beneficiary.

In October 1964 Old Woody was arrested for vagrancy in Richmond. Allowed only one phone call, he used it to notify CIA of his plight. A couple of weeks later he phoned to report his new motorcycle license, and still later he wrote that he was working on a boat in Miami. Back in the money early in 1965, he wrote from Bermuda that he had been appointed King of the British Empire.

The risk of arrest did not dampen Old Woody's enthusiasm for the service. In August 1960 he made a telephone appointment with the commanding officer of an Air Force base in Nevada, conducted a "CIA security inspection," used the base commander's telephone to call CIA headquarters in Washington, and on departure warned the commander that some officers were out of uniform at Harold's Club. After sending MP's on a wild goose chase to the gambling club, the base commander somewhat grumpily reported the incident in an official letter to CIA. A few months later Old Woody was not so lucky. In Ponce, Puerto Rico, he represented himself as an FBI agent, borrowed a jeep from the National Guard, and drove it across the island to San Juan, where he was arrested. "Dear Allen," he wrote from jail, "I am in trouble again." A few days later he grew petulant. "You are wasting your time and the Armed Forces' time," he wrote, "I do not intend a reconciliation."

Generous to a fault, Old Woody rented a Cadillac limousine and chauffeur at $100 a day just before Christmas 1960 and drove to the Soviet embassy, where he left $100 for Francis Gary Powers. Then he drove to the Cuban embassy with $100 for prisoners on the Isle of Pines, and then to the American Red Cross, where he contributed $70 to help unmarried mothers. Finally he came to CIA headquarters and handed the receptionist an envelope addressed to Mr. Dulles containing $50 as a Christmas present. These activities landed him in St. Elizabeth's Hospital, from which he escaped a few days later after getting back the $50 from CIA. But he was pleased with the episode; nearly two years later he wrote Mr. Dulles that "some day I'll give you another $50 bill as a token of my affection."

In November 1961 he wrote from El Paso: "When the new Director takes over, I guess I'll wash my hands of CIA." But Old Woody didn't, and the flow of letters continued. In December 1961 he put down CIA as his home address when he opened a bank account in Wilmington, Delaware. In October 1962 he telegraphed from Chicago: "FIDEL CASTRO MINUS HIS BEARD ARRIVED CHICAGO THIS P.M. HAVE DETAIL COVERING HIM." In September 1963 a Washington-Miami airliner turned back and off-loaded him; he had alarmed fellow passengers by claiming to be a personal friend of Fidel Castro and trying to communicate with CIA by radio.

Is Old Woody just a harmless screwball? In 1960 he wrote: "Allen, I am going to start carrying a regulation FBI revolver and if someone forces me into a situation I intend on using it." In 1961 he warned Mr. Dulles: "The bomb attached to my radio in Room 313 has not availed you anything so far." Who knows what Old Woody will interpret as "a situation"? At a minimum, he has cost the Government a great many dollars in wasted time, filing space, analysis, and precautions. As he himself put it in a 1960 letter from West Palm Beach: "Allen, you should deduct me from your income tax."

Fish and a Record

Some crank correspondents are remarkably well educated and successful in business or the arts. Take the 50-year-old daughter of a high-ranking Army officer who now owns a prosperous small town shop. Educated in Europe and widely travelled, she served abroad with the Red Cross in World War II and has written many successful books including one which was made into a major motion picture. She writes beautifully and, at first glance, convincingly.

It was the fish that gave her away. Her early letters just asked for information about an inner circle of Government officials who used a drawing of a fish as the symbol of "a confidentially shared community of patriotic attitude." Then she started sending CIA officials postcards with crude drawings of fish. Later she adopted the fish as a signature to her own letters.

In 1962 the fish-woman asked the vice president of a Washington bank to help finance a small private counterespionage organization working to expose "the mammoth traitorous operation at present flourishing within our Government." Meanwhile she wrote threatening anonymous letters, mailed them to herself, and then forwarded them to CIA to prove the existence of a conspiracy. Ignored for years, she continues writing long and quite articulate letters. The most recent one, mailed in March 1965, contains roughly 11,000 words.

One might think that if no one answered their letters the crank correspondents would eventually get discouraged and quit writing. This is not always true. CIA's most faithful correspondent has been plugging a single theme steadily since 1951, when he decided a "CIA agent" had welshed on a job offer. Almost every day he mails a postcard with the same message: "Take Action on CIA Agent Joe Blank!" He has been arrested and released on his promise to stop writing; within a few days the postcards arrive again. He has written from Miami, Las Vegas, San Francisco, Phoenix, Denver, Rochester, Colorado Springs, and Hampton, Va.—hitting his peak in 1962 with a total of 332 postcards to CIA. He has also carried his complaint to the Secretary of Defense, but a special assistant at the Pentagon politely suggested in reply that he deal directly with CIA.

Violence

Are such cranks actually dangerous? Read on.

On 13 March 1963 a "consulting nuclear engineer" called at CIA's downtown personnel office and tried to see the DCI. File checks showed that four years earlier he had sent the Director a letter marked "DEATH" and signed "Lord God, God of Israel." On 28 October 1958 he had hired a taxi in Richmond, picked up two hitchhikers and a 9-year-old boy, and tried to invade the Quantico Marine Corps School brandishing the boy's toy pistols.

The night of 21 February 1962 a man who thought he was a CIA agent telephoned four times trying to report to the Director. On 11 November 1962 the same man was arrested in Rapid City, S.D., after terrorizing residential areas of that city, firing dozens of shots through windows, and wounding one resident. When arrested he was carrying a high-powered rifle, a .22-caliber rifle, and a large quantity of ammunition.

One crank has been bombarding more than 50 top Government officials with details of alleged Communist electronic thought-control by "a coherent light process of inducing a state of controlled hypnosis by radiation of radio frequency energy on a wavelength of approximately 4 x 10^{-5} centimeters." The writer is officially diagnosed as a paranoiac schizophrenic, potentially dangerous.

On 12 December 1964 a 53-year-old Florida real estate salesman mailed the DCI a crude threat note ending "Your card is the ACE OF SPADES." This man had tried to see the Director in the past—once to discuss a proposed trip to Russia, again to report his invention of the hardest metal in the world. He is diagnosed as a chronic schizophrenic paranoiac with "delusions of grandeur, seclusiveness, and hostility" who should be kept in a "structured and supervised setting." He was arrested three times in 1964, once for carrying a concealed weapon. Earlier he had been arrested for armed robbery and in 1960 in Arlington, Va., for attempted murder.

In 1962, with the arrival of a new DCI, CIA informally reviewed protective measures with Secret Service and Metropolitan Police Department officers. It was reaffirmed that, while the threat of an attack on top Agency officials was unpredictable and might never materialize, it was nevertheless real enough to require professional protection. Events since then have underlined this view, although there has been no (knock on wood) actual injury. Probably the closest call was when a woman wrestler traced one top official to the home of relatives and lunged at him with a bouquet of roses which was afterwards found to hide a jagged broken beer bottle.

In any intelligence agency it is important to keep track of crank contacts, not only to improve protection but also to assure continuity of control and analysis. Centralization of records in CIA's Office of Security permits quick identification of phonies and time-wasters. Professional security officers know how to handle the off-beat approach, and others would do well to rely on the professionals when they receive an irrational letter or find themselves face to face with an apparently unbalanced stranger.

OFFICE OF THE DNI

A visit to the headquarters of the Office of the Director of National Intelligence will find these posters, based upon the popular Despair commercially-available series of posters, plastered on various walls. The format is a striking photo, followed by a one- or two-word ALL CAPS title, and a snarky annotation:

// 🌐 //

*14<har*_2Tli!9Sp@$Wk#(rD5*
COMPUTER SECURITY
Because, sometimes, the best security is to keep everyone out.

Washington crossing the Delaware
OPSEC
"Even minutiae should have a place in our collection, for things of a seemingly trifling nature when employed with others of a more serious cast may lead to valuable conclusions."—George Washington, ca 1776

// ⊕ //

F-14 flying
AIRSPACE
It's ours. We'll give it back to you when we're done with it.

// ⊕ //

Photo of James Jesus Angleton, head of CIA's Counterintelligence office
ANGLETON
"Paranoia strikes deep; into your mind it will creep."
—"For What It's Worth," by Buffalo Springfield

// ⊕ //

Photo of Army officer, with overweight guy in an Army t-shirt in background
STRONG
There's Strong. Then there's Army Strong.
Lucky for us, we still have Marines.

// ⊕ //

Guys wading, shirtless, in freezing water, carrying carbines
MANLINESS
Does there have to be a better reason?

// ⊕ //

Crashed helicopter
CHINA
Our best hope is that they're even dumber than we are.

German Shepherd with helmet and AK47 around its neck
THE PEOPLE'S ARMED POLICE
The junior varsity of China

// ⊕ //

CLOUDS
Annoying the **** out of imagery analysts since World War I

// ⊕ //

Tony Soprano
COUNTERINTELLIGENCE
There's only one way to deal with a rat, and if you do it right, all the other rats and would-be rats get the message.

// ⊕ //

ANA MONTES
She was the DIA's leading Cuba analyst…
but she was also Cuba's leading DIA analyst.

// ⊕ //

Gorilla looking irritated, with arms crossed
DISCLOSURE REQUESTS
What part of "no" don't they understand?

// ⊕ //

Parachute leaving plane
CREDIT
Slamming your eyes shut and pissing your pants on exit does not count as a night water jump in your jump log.

Male lion
ARROGANCE
The best leaders inspire by example.
When that's not an option, brute intimidation works pretty well, too.

Guy in camo, sacked out on a camo couch
CAMOUFLAGE
Protecting men from honey-do's since 1902

CENTCOM
punking jihad since 1983

F-16 photo
CHINESE F-16 DECOYS
What better way to keep the imperialists from bombing your airfield than to make them think they've already overrun it and commenced flight operations?

Penguin holding cymbals, standing on top of sleeping polar bear
COURAGE
Do one brave thing today…then run like hell.

Guy in witch costume
DENIAL AND DECEPTION
Then again, D&D might just stand for "Dungeons and Dragons"

Cyclops
NOFORN
Sometimes one eye is enough
(*Ed's note:* classification meaning No Foreigners can have access)

// 🌐 //

DREAMS
Dreams are like rainbows. Only idiots chase them

// 🌐 //

Horse sniffing another's ****
FLATTERY
If you want to get to the top, prepare to kiss a lot of the bottom.

// 🌐 //

Tired leopard
INDIFFERENCE
It takes 43 muscles to frown and 17 to smile, but it doesn't take any to just sit there with a dumb look on your face.

// 🌐 //

Snowflakes
INDIVIDUALITY
Always remember that you are unique. Just like everybody else.

// 🌐 //

Giant and tiny dogs stare-down
INTIMIDATION
No one can make you feel inferior without your consent, but you'd be a fool to withhold that from your superiors.

Eagle soaring
LEADERS
Leaders are like eagles. We don't have either of them here.

// 🌐 //

One knife-sharpened pencil amongst unsharpened ones
PLANNING
Much work remains to be done before we can announce our total failure to make any progress.

// 🌐 //

STRIFE
As long as we have each other,
we'll never run out of problems.

// 🌐 //

Growing snowball rolling downhill
TEAMWORK
A few harmless flakes working together
can unleash an avalanche of destruction.

// 🌐 //

ALL SOURCE ANALYSTS
Called that because they try to do it "all" by themselves

// 🌐 //

THE CIA
If it was a stock, and we were your broker,
we'd be telling you to sell.

"The Scream" painting
THE D&D COMMUNITY
Its products tend to provoke this sort of reaction throughout the IC.

// 🌐 //

The DIA
Ever wonder why they say
"Military intelligence is a contradiction in terms"?
(*Ed's note:* Defense Intelligence Agency)

// 🌐 //

YOU FAIL AT FAILING.
No, that's not a double negative.

// 🌐 //

Keystone Kops
THE FBI
Don't worry. The Bureau has things under control.

// 🌐 //

FIREPOWER
If it's not working, you're not using enough

// 🌐 //

FIRE SUPPORT
The Marquess of Queensberry never had to go door-to-door in dispersed tactical formation, with multiple engagement zones and the threat of recurring lateral ambushes.

GEOINT
OK. And the punch line is…?
(*Ed's note:* Geospatial Intelligence)

// 🌐 //

IMINT
People used to look at it with awe until Google Earth ruined everything.
(*Ed's note:* Imagery Intelligence)

// 🌐 //

INFINITE RECURSION
You gotta know when to quit.

// 🌐 //

Monopoly's moneybags man
THE INR
Elitists? Oh, no, not the State Department!
(*Ed's note:* Bureau of Intelligence and Research)

// 🌐 //

MASINT
We don't know what the hell it is either.
(*Ed's note:* Measurement and Signature Intelligence)

// 🌐 //

Gomer Pyle
THE MCIA
The few, the proud, the frequently inaccurate
(*Ed's note:* Marine Corps Intelligence Activity)

// 🌐 //

Three Stooges
THE NASIC
It's part of the Air Force,
but it isn't exactly advertising that fact these days.
(*Ed's note:* National Air and Space Intelligence Center)

// ⊕ //

THE NCS
The part of the CIA that perpetually needs
"five years to rebuild our HUMINT capabilities"
(*Ed's note:* National Clandestine Service)

// ⊕ //

Nerd
NGA
In 2003, NIMA thought a three-letter abbreviation would make it cool.
It was mistaken.
(*Ed's note:* National Imagery and Mapping Agency which became
National Geospatial Intelligence Agency)

// ⊕ //

Three rednecks
THE NGIC
The best darn intelligence agency America has
….in Charlottesville, Virginia
(*Ed's note:* National Ground Intelligence Center)

// ⊕ //

THE NIC
It's that part of the ODNI that writes those great reports
the policy makers ignore.
(*Ed's note:* National Intelligence Council)

Crusty the Clown
THE NRO
People there drive the satellites. No, we're not kidding.
(*Ed's note:* National Reconnaissance Office)

// 🌐 //

Three nerds
THE NSA
The geeks, dweebs, nerds and doofuses you used to beat up in high school are now listening to all your telephone calls.
(*Ed's note:* National Security Agency)

// 🌐 //

Egyptian pyramids
THE ODNI
Because the IC can always use more layers of managers.
(*Ed's note:* Office of the Director of National Intelligence)

// 🌐 //

Animal baring teeth
THE ONCIX
Their investigators just want to have a friendly chat with you.
(*Ed's note:* Office of the National Counterintelligence Executive)

// 🌐 //

Sinking ship
THE ONI
Unlike the NCIS, nobody's likely to make a television show about it since sitcoms rarely succeed.
(*Ed's note:* Office of Naval Intelligence)

// 🌐 //

Rodney Dangerfield
OSINT
It doesn't get any respect, either.
(*Ed's note:* Open Source Intelligence)

// ⊕ //

POLYGRAPHERS
Ever wonder who the descendants of the Spanish Inquisition are?

// ⊕ //

VLADIMIR PUTIN
He put the "cagey" into KGB

// ⊕ //

Water cooler
RUMINT
Disseminated around the world before SIGINT can put on its shoes.
(*Ed's note:* Rumor Intelligence doesn't formally exist, but everyone believes it. SIGINT: Signals Intelligence)

// ⊕ //

The Joker
SOCOM
Their operatives frequently have a very strange idea of what constitutes "plainclothes."
(*Ed's note:* Special Operations Command)

// ⊕ //

Guy in a tiny boat, with a 50-caliber machine gun
COAST GUARD ICC
Doing the best with what we have!

3 ayatollahs saying: "That was pathetic. You sounded like Satan singing karaoke. Jihad on you, your friends, and your entire family."
IRANIAN IDOL
Makes Simon look like a pussycat.

// ⊕ //

FINANCIAL D&D
You can steal more with a briefcase than with a gun.

// ⊕ //

Che t-shirt
REVOLUTIONARIES
Even if you spend your whole life combating the forces of capitalism, you still might wind up on a t-shirt sold in a store owned by the Gap.

// ⊕ //

The Office of the DNI is often the topic of jokes by the rest of the members of the Intelligence Community. One particularly popular one: Why does the DNI logo have 50 stars? One for each Associate Deputy Director.

Sometimes there is downtime when conducting surveillance or waiting for editors to mangle one's prose. An IC wag asked "How do you fight apathy when/if it enters into your daily life?" Among the answers:

- If you can fake it, having a good attitude the next day sometimes fools you into a better mood. If it doesn't fool you, at least you're not depressing everyone around you.
- I don't care. (Oh, come on. You Know everyone was thinking it!)
- Active Retirement Planning!

- It's not My apathy I seem to be fighting.
- I'm the guy who does his job. You must be the other guy.
- I come to work and sit in on captivating meetings, where we discuss planning meetings about…meetings! What could be better?!
- Let's ask the other 99% of the readers who read but did not respond to the article!
- When someone's apathetic, I take some of their stuff. That generally gets them going.
- They held an Apathy Convention last year but it was cancelled due to lack of interest! (*Ed's note:* I never promised that these would be original…)

The Office of the DNI offers this simple guide to interpreting intellicrat-speak:

TERM	MEANING
Data Point	a guess
Significant challenges exist	It's completely messed up
Rough order of magnitude	Totally made up off-the-cuff
I haven't heard it expressed in that manner	That's bogus
Here's the way ahead	Here's a list of futile taskers
Our analytical rigor has not been completed	We are making stuff up
Let's talk about it offline	Shut up
We have a customized solution	It's going to be crazy expensive
I'm happy to show you our detailed analysis	Care for some public humiliation?

BE CAREFUL WHERE YOU TURN

Ed's note: Mark Ingham, a visiting Canadian, offered this story in a Toastmasters humor speech contest. He won.

Has anyone here driven in Washington, DC? Did you get lost? (*Wrong answer!* Or *Me, too.*)

Washington, DC is the most confusing city in the world. Only locals know their way around. It's a national security thing, an invading army would be hopelessly lost.

So, I persuaded my college to let me take a vanload of freshman on a tour of their national capital.

I am a Canadian. Therefore, we got lost.

After many miles on a freeway into Langley, VA, we see our first exit! A HUGE Freeway sign *[hold up sign]*:

You laugh? We laughed too. *[alternately: Can you believe it, some of the Americans in the van laughed!]*

Authorized Vehicles only?

I've no recollection. This sign was tacked up after what happened to me! Small, unmatched, obviously an afterthought.

We had wasted so much time already. I wanted to make the trip worthwhile.

Maybe we could get a tour of the CIA headquarters?

The worst that could happen is that we have to make a u-turn.

It isn't until I am on the one way road into the compound that I see a small sign tacked to a tree that says: "authorized vehicles only."

A one way DIVIDED road. No u-turn.

So, I am this foreign national. *[Hold up Picture—I've long hair. Hold up second picture: beard, bandana]*

I am driving an unmarked van, tinted windows, the license plate says "virtue" in GREEK. This was a few months after 9-11 AND there had recently been a shootup at this very entrance!

I come around a corner and there is what looks like a border-crossing building of reflective bullet-proof glass arching over the road.

I pull up to the intercom. After a very long silence:

"State your business."

"Um, ahh, I'm from St. John's College. I guess we made a wrong turn. We were out and about trying to park by the Lincoln Memorial. Can we just turn around?"

Another long silence.

Finally, that voice, dead serious: "proceed slowly forward to the approaching officer."

Faintly, in the background, we heard laughter.

The glass opened. A 6 foot 4, 230 lb. muscle-bound man in uniform emerged—his hand tensely poised at his gun.

I proceeded "slowly forward to the approaching officer."

"Put the vehicle in Park."

"Turn off the engine."

"Do you know where you are?"

"Um, the George Bush Center for Intelligence." (I did keep a straight face, honest.)

"Uh Huh."

"We were wondering if we could get a tour?"

"Uh uh."

"I need identification for everyone in the vehicle."

I passed him my student card.

"Your STATE Identification!"

"Um, Province?" I gave him my Manitoba driver's license along with 10 other IDs.

"How many cameras in the vehicle?"

"Aaah, three."

"Did anyone take any pictures on the way in?"

"Oh, no."

"Did anyone take any pictures on the way in?"

"Alright."

The glass opened. A woman came out. This was the scariest human being I have ever seen! Nothing in particular about her stood out. I mean she wasn't ugly or monstrous, but the look on her face meant business!

The "approaching officer" met her half way just out of earshot. I was so relieved, she never came any closer.

They radio'd our ID's into Headquarters one by one.

The glass opened. Another man came out with a large black box on his belt. Slowly, he walked towards us, putting on tight black leather gloves. They called him off just before he got to the van. I still wonder, what was he about to do?

They took our IDs into the building.

Now we were alone. We looked around. We were not alone.

We were surrounded by armored men with machine guns and shotguns and boxed in by a squad car.

There was silence in the van.

Finally someone said: "They took our IDs, does somebody have something on them?"

(I'm thinking to myself, 'this is the CIA, I'm a bearded foreign national, I've lived in the Middle East, I've been to Cuba, I arrived in this country within days of 9/11…")

Someone said: "I bet they are listening to us."

Silence.

"Well, what should we say, then."

Everyone started giggling!

After a very long time of awkward comments, the glass opened, the officer approached, gave me the stack of IDs.

"If you ever come back here, you are liable for indictment for Trespassing on Federal Property. Now, I want you to drive up to that intersection, stop, shoulder check, if it is clear, proceed to your left. When you get to the entrance, wait for the light, turn left, and follow the signs to go back to DC."

There was this freshman sitting behind me, one of those really macho frat boy types. At each pronouncement, Chris piped in: "Yes, officer, yes, officer."

I thanked the officer, and then I asked: "While we are up here, is there anything else we could see?"

He looked at me: "Uh uh."

"Well, actually, officer, I saw a sign for some sort of Animal Farm."

The guy finally relaxed for just a moment and said, "Oh, that, yeah, so, if you take a right at the entrance, the road will take you down to the petting zoo. But it's Sunday, and they are probably closed."

"Oh, okay, I guess we'll just go back to DC then."

At the end of the day, my freshman presented me with a CIA toque. Of course, being Americans, they called it a "hat."

So, fellow toastmasters, when you read a huge American Exit sign, always look for the fine print!

A GUIDE TO THE DENIZENS OF THE INTELLIGENCE COMMUNITY FAMILY

In *The Secret Book of CIA Humor*, we looked at how CIA's analytic offices were like high school cliques. Not to be outdone, the members of the Intelligence Community compared themselves to members of a dysfunctional family. They took their cue from Agent Lowry, in Conspiracy Theory, who observed, "If the Intelligence Community is a family, think of us as the uncle nobody wants to talk about."

Director of National Intelligence (DNI)
- The ineffective mom whom none of the kids ever listens to.
- But everyone sort of has to listen to sometimes, when they need money.

Department of Defense (DoD)
- DoD is Dad, then
- Never around when you need him?

- He says "ask your mother" when he doesn't want to be bothered.
- Always off "warfighting" no time to worry about day-in day-out around the house business.
- But he won't let her make any real decisions.
- And then gets all angry when the family does something embarrassing.
- The Policymaker and the Warfighter are the deadbeat dad who left when the oldest kid was 10, and who all the other kids have psychologically tried to please ever since.

Congress
- Congress is the rich uncle everybody kisses up to.
- But no one likes cause he smells funny. And leers at the babysitter
- Or that Mom occasionally sleeps with, when the family needs money.
- He can always find some special gift for his favorite kids

Central Intelligence Agency (CIA)
- …as I once said to Jack Kennedy whilst yachting one day…
- CIA would be the Know-It-All of the family who likes to keep secrets from everyone else while trying to get up into everyone else's business.
- CIA is the uncle who is a Vietnam vet who gets into fights and is arrested a lot and always tells.
- CIA is the oldest brother. He went to Harvard, so Mom and Dad like him best.

National Security Agency (NSA)
- Ummm, Dad? We really need a stronger password for the wi-fi encryption.
- NSA would be the crazy old uncle with a long beard who wears a tinfoil hat.

- If NSA was a person, it would have some kind of pill addiction.
- Who only looks at peoples' shoes.
- No, it's the nerdy brother who gets good grades but never bathes.

National Geospatial-Intelligence Agency (NGA)
- Son, I am disappointed.
- NGA is the "entrepreneurial" younger brother who always has some neat get-rich scheme so he can prove to Dad that he's just as good as his elder siblings.

Defense Intelligence Agency (DIA)
- Was once left at a rest stop while on a family trip.
- DIA is that one kid whose birthday always gets skipped.
- Yeah…DIA is the one who people mention at the end and everyone goes "oh, yeah…them"
- Like Jermaine?
- "The middle child"

National Reconnaissance Office (NRO)
- Look, Mom! I spent the mortgage money on these Monster Cables!
- So is NRO the embarrassing relative who has a reputation as the family's "peeping Tom"?
- NRO, the car salesman who always charges extra for every feature possible
- Lately it feels like NRO is more like the car manufacturer who's asked to create a Tesla on a Prius budget.

Office of Naval Intelligence (ONI)
- The one with the boat.

National Air and Space Intelligence Center (NASIC)
- The one that makes model airplanes

National Ground Intelligence Center (NGIC)
- The one that melted his Army Men
- The Service Intelligence Agencies are the bratty grandkids who always fight over which toy belongs to whom.
- "Mom! He's on my side of the car again!"
- And you always end up paying extra to buy the same toys for each one of them

There are separate ways to tell the different types of military services. This version looks at how they deal with the rain and what they have to say about it:

Infantry: This sucks.

Ranger: I like that this sucks.

Special Forces: I wish this sucked more.

Close Air Support: It looks like it sucks down there.

Marines: Embrace the suck.

Intelligence Officer, clicking his TV remote in his living room while it rains outside: The storm knocked out my cable; this sucks.

TRAINING

I was teaching a group of Operations Center officers, examining the idiosyncrasies of English. After discussing all the problems with pronouns, exceptions to the rules, etc., I said to the class at least in English by far the most common way to form a plural is to put an "s" on the end of the noun. A few minutes later one of the students blurted out, "What is the plural of octopus?" In order to prevent a law suit against me, I answered "calamari."

When the Agency went to the PAR system in which employees had to write about themselves, I was asked to design a one-day work shop to teach people how to write to a set of objectives without appearing to brag. The first couple of years I was busy all the time. I was teaching at one of the Agency's out-buildings. On the first floor there is a small cafeteria. I would come down every morning for my coffee and got to know the young man who was the cashier—very nice, but a 40 watt light bulb. I had been teaching there three weeks in a row when he said, "Man, you are here all the time!" I responded, "Yes, I am swamped with work and just look at each day as another day in the teaching orgasmatron." The next day when I went to pay, he leaned over and asked, "What kind of equipment do you use in your class?" I was left speechless. When I told a friend the story, he said why didn't you say, "I have one under each student's chair and turn it one periodically during the class." I wish I could think of those comebacks.

During rookie operations training, we try to get the students to pick meeting sites that do not attract attention. Alas, I've had students choose the following sites:

- **A used car lot.** While this sounds good in principle—you can loiter if needed while waiting for someone—weather can play havoc with outdoor sites. As it did when a student had me wait in the pouring rain for him, while a bevy of used car salesmen braved the torrent to ask me if I really, really wanted to look at their cars.

- **A small building in a compound.** Normally a decent locale, the student didn't know that the building was to be demolished an hour before we were to meet.

- **A restaurant.** Certainly a natural place to meet, perhaps not that good if you need to talk very sensitive issues and you're not absolutely sure of how the interlocutor will react. During the recruitment phrase of the course, we instructors knew that the students were going to try to "pitch" us. So I went to the restaurant ahead of time, and told the waitstaff that I was an out-of-work actor who would be meeting with this young, hotshot producer. The producer might ask me to read for a part during the meal, so if I was raising my voice and gesticulating wildly, it was merely a part. They told me they were solidly behind my efforts, and would support me however I needed. So we sit down to the meal, and when the student pitched me, I jumped on the table and said "You want me to do What? For the C-I-A!" Never did tell the waitstaff whether I got the part...

- **Again, stay away from restaurants.** I'd been asked to meet with a student who had been particularly self-impressed, and thought he knew everything. So I put on my favorite flashy-blond outfit and sat down to our meeting with him. Unbeknownst to our all-knowing student, I had my office-mate, also a flashy blond, show up and yell at me: "What are you doing with this, this...man! I thought we had something special when we marched in Sunday's Gay Pride march. But now This!" and stormed off. I then ran off a few paces behind her, leaving the student in the middle of scores of fascinated stares.

- **A bookstore:** Another fine place to loiter, but make sure that you tell them the correct bookstore. I've loitered many an extra minute because the student did not know that there were two bookstores in the mall. (For those readers who are a little bit younger, before there was Amazon, there were things called bookstores, where you could buy things called books.) In another instance, a student told me to wait for him in a bookstore and hold a napkin as a physical "the coast is clear" sign. I did precisely what he told me to do, and merrily handed him a sanitary napkin.

WHAT THE SUPPORT FOLKS HAVE TO DEAL WITH

I was serving as the finance officer at a station when a case officer stopped by and asked if he could see one million of the local currency. I asked him if he wanted to sign out one million of the currency. He said, "no, I just need to see it. There's a very tough customs check at the border crossing, and I need to bring one million across the border for a meeting I'm having with an asset. So I'm going to stuff the currency in my underwear. I want to see that much cash, to see if it will fit." When I showed him the million, he said that would easily fit. I had him sign a receipt, and asked that he not bring back any change.

// ⊕ //

Numerous support staffs across the Intelligence Community host suggestion boxes, blogs, complaint boards, etc., to obtain employee input. Here are some outtakes:

A policy recently came out stating all government employees traveling greater than 50 miles from their home and spending the night must notify their office by submitting specifics on the travel using a spreadsheet. This should occur preferably prior to the travel taking place but should be reported even if after the fact. It was further explained that this is being mandated by the Director. Is this true? I have an issue with this request and believe it gets too far into what employees do when away from work. It's like our organization wishes to constantly keep tabs on the workforce.

I understand the need for accountability but not at this level. I personally believe this new requirement in the name of accountability is not only intrusive, but I question the legality of forcing employees to comply. *(This was followed by the following postings.)*

- Am I supposed to let NGA know every time I spend the night with my girlfriend? What if my wife finds out?
- I wonder if I need to report myself daily, because I live 80 miles from work and I sleep over there every night. I better get started on my Excel spreadsheet.
- My first entry in the Employee Whereabouts Tracker: Dear Director, I never thought this would happen to a guy like me. I was driving back from a fishing trip from the lake on August 25. I was in a small rural town about 52 miles from my home when there was a loud clunk and some smoke coming from the engine compartment of my truck. Fortunately for me, I could see a gas station in the distance. By the time I reached the garage I was dripping with sweat. The sign said Mechanic on Duty: Sam. I didn't see anyone, so I called out. Sir….nothing. Sam…nothing. Then she walked out…with dark blue overalls with a little name tag that said Sam. I could tell by the look in her eye…there wasn't much else on under the overalls and this repair was going to cost me.

// ⊕ //

I have received numerous reports that there are birds flying in the Atrium. Please be aware that these are really not birds. They are really an "NGA Prototype Stealth "Boid" Drone" (NPSBD for short). This NPSBD drone has a micro-mini camera for an eye. The NPSBD cruises the length and breadth of the Atrium to observe and collect target data for analysis by the support service staff (aka Da Kooks). Data analysis is used to determine what to serve and who is getting served. If by chance you are selected as a trackable target, you will be blessed with a small white spot that is really a miniature GPS tracking device that is used to track you and record where you go throughout the facility… so Da Kooks know where you are taking "da food".

Now that I have your attention, I need to ask for your assistance.

Our pest control services contract has been attempting to capture the birds in various locations throughout the building but with very limited success. It appears that there are groups of employees that like to feed the birds and thus the birds are not hungry enough to eat the food in the capture cages. We now have to expand the effort with the placement of more capture cages in more common areas. Please be aware we will be randomly placing capture cages in the West end of the Atrium from 1900 to 0400. The cages will have food and water and will be removed with the surrounding areas cleaned prior to morning arrival for the majority of occupants. Any birds captured will be released back to their natural habitat. The duration of this effort will depend on how long it takes the birds to become comfortable with the capture cages/traps so that they are attracted by the food and willingly enter the trap/cage.

What can you do to help? One way to hasten our release of the birds back outside to their natural habitat would be refrain from providing additional food for them while eating. We are focused on the safe capture and release of the birds. Your assistance in this matter will be most appreciated.

I have seen emails stating that the birds we had in the Atrium were being caught and released unharmed. We have a mouse problem in my office space, and the traps they are using are the traditional kind that are designed to snap the vertebra of the mice. Isn't there a way to capture them without killing them? Why care for the life of the birds and not for the life of the mice? (*Ed's note:* this note generated the following responses)

- Is this person volunteering to let all captured mice come live at his/her house?
- We caught and released one mouse, but another one was killed in the traps set by the pest control people in our workspace. Apparently birds are wildlife, but mice are pests.
- What about all of the insects killed by poisons, traps, and shoes? We never hear about those poor creatures. And no one sheds a tear when a carrot or tomato is massacred just so we humans can eat lunch!

- I suggest a mouse adoption booth be set up at Family Day.
- Brilliant! A few tips—naming animals always makes them more relate-able. Also, I suggest colored bows or shawls to dress them up a bit. Maybe we can convince the ASPCA to get on board to certify our facility after the event so we can be even more than just LEED certified.
- I have always wanted to be a professional animal namer. Now my dream can finally be realized.
- You could get it put on your NGA business cards!
- I think the birds (like old people) have a more powerful lobby in Washington than the rodents (like young people). That is why it is illegal to discriminate against persons with advanced age, but rental car, insurance, and credit card companies can discriminate against younger people.

// ⊕ //

We wish to take this opportunity to thank you all for your support and understanding during our "suspicious package" event this AM. The event was a response to a vibrating noise emanating from a trash can outside the elevator bank on the first floor of the garage. The event tested our emergency response system, and we are glad that it as a false alarm. In short, the NGA Protective Services Police, Emergency Management Team, the Fort Belvoir Police and the Explosive Ordnance Disposal Team, only to name a few, performed admirably. Your cooperation during the event was also a strong contributing factor to the successful conclusion of the event. The post event "hot wash" gave us another opportunity to review our procedures, identify deficiencies, and address corrective actions to ensure that we are better prepared to respond to any emergency on the site. Again, thank you.

PS: And as Paul Harvey would say, "Now for the rest of the story…" In the future, if you have a need to dispose of a battery-operated device, please remove the batteries first. In this case, the noise was caused by the vibrations of a battery-operated toothbrush.

// ⊕ //

During a routine cell/laptop/notebook locker inspection it was noted that the items in several of the laptop/notebook computer lockers would fit into the smaller cellphone locker. There are 1392 cellphone lockers and only 140 laptop/notebook lockers at the NCE. To ensure that the laptop/notebook lockers are available to those that need them, I respectfully request that you store your smaller items in the smaller lockers. Yes, size does make a difference. (I knew that title would get your attention…)

Now for the rest of the story. For those that store their lunches and other food stuffs in the cellphone/laptop lockers, I need to request that you stop this practice since some of its gets very ripe and becomes a full-blown science experiment if it is forgotten. We do have refrigerators in the pantries and cafes for those who wish to store their lunch.

With that said, here is a reminder for those that do use the refrigerators in the cafes and pantries. Please take a look through the refrigerators that you are using. My last look/see came up with a yogurt with a use-by date of 7 months ago, a milk container that had something solid in it that used to be milk, another had an empty ice cream container, and yet another with something that Alfred Hitchcock would have difficulty describing. Many of the refrigerators were over-packed with very little space remaining. Please take the time to free up some of the space by removing the expired items to make room for future science experiments.

// ⊕ //

Topic du Jour—Animals on Federal Facilities

Just as a reminder, there is a prohibition for having animals on federal facilities. The only exception provided is for trained and certified service animals accompanied by their owner/handler. Besides dogs and cats, gerbils, hamsters, frogs, turtles, birds, reptiles, insects, and fish, etc., are all considered animals. This prohibition derives its roots from various laws and regulations in both the security and health arenas. In NGA, you can find the animal prohibition on the prohibited items list.

As I have previously noted, you are a very creative workforce and in each of my walks throughout the facility little things come to my attention. To that end, I must respectfully ask that all of the terrariums (with insects, spiders, and the like in them), ant farms, and fish bowls (aka aquariums) be removed from the facility. If the terrarium or ant farm is actually the result of a lunch or snack experiment gone bad, please call 7-1111 and we can arrange for a certified pest controller and/or custodian to assist in the removal.

As for the birds in the Atrium, we work each case separately for a safe and humanitarian removal.

If, per chance, I see you walking with a little fish on the end of a leash with a blue service animal vest on it, I will not question the certification of the fish as a service animal, but I may question you on where the fish was trained, and why you are not wearing a snorkel and fins.

In short, I ask you to please remove ant farms and fish bowls/tanks, from the facility.

I've heard a lot in my time but this one cuts into new territory. In a former assignment as a fire marshal I experienced dumpster fires, coal mine fires, landfill fires, building fires, car fires and even forest fires. All could be attributable to a known cause.

The inevitable has happened. All I can say is that somehow a tree, a single tree, in the "middle of nowhere" by the West Atrium patio "self-ignited." This "self-igniting" tree is between the area where the BBQ grills are located and where many smokers congregate in lieu of the area directly around the Smoking Shelter where smoking is authorized. Not that I doubt that this tree and the mulch around it "self-ignited", but since it did I must request the following:

- Please, if you are a smoker, smoke only in the designated place in the vicinity of the Smoking Shelter.
- Please use the appropriate cigarette disposal containers.
- Please, do not extinguish your cigarette butts in the grass or mulch surrounding the trees.
- Please, if you are using the BBQ trailers, deposit any embers/ashes in the appropriate metal containers.
- Lastly, if you see any more of the newly-planted trees "self-igniting" or any fire, call 911 to report it.

(*Ed's note:* I can't seem to recall James Bond having this kind of problem when he smoked.)

Department of Wet (paint) Works

There is an ongoing maintenance program to paint areas in need of touchup or complete repainting. The process includes repair of "dings", a little drywall mud, maybe a little sanding, and some primer, then the paint. This is a big building and the crews are doing quite a bit of touchup painting. The painters are quite proud of their work and try to do the best job they can.

Now the reason for this note:

The Wet Paint signs that are placed in the area being worked mean "WET Paint". For all of those with paint on their fingertips (I know many of you are looking at your fingertips while you read this), I apologize. Please trust me on this, when the crew applies the paint, it is WET… That is why they put up the signs. As evidenced by the number of spots that are requiring additional touchup after the painters do the initial repainting, many of you are in the "Trust but Verify" mode.

I need to ask you to please, refrain from your own personal Quality Assurance inspection. The painting crew will remove the "Wet Paint" signs when the paint is dry and suitable for the "touch" test. Thank you in advance for your support. (This generated the following responses.)

- I just wanted to see what their definition of "wet" was.
- First, I'm happy to know that the painters are proud of their work. Good for them. Second, we have so many acronyms around here that I lose track. Can someone help me? What does WET stand for again?
- That's on a need-to-know basis.
- Want Everyone to Touch (WET)
- If you really want to tell if the paint is dry, lick it.

AN EARLY BRUSH WITH FAME

By Rob Kresge

In the early 1970s when I was a newbie assigned to the Foreign Broadcast Information Service (FBIS) as a foreign press analyst, I worked for some months with a Bill Barr in one of the tall office buildings in Roslyn, Virginia. We had both been hired as GS-8s. Bill lived in a high rise apartment building across one street from our offices.

Less than six months in, we were both summoned one day to a senior FBIS officer's office and were told that the Agency would no longer be filling our positions with GS-8s and we were hereby promoted to GS-9s. We looked at each other and walked out in a daze. All right, two dazes.

When we were walking back to our bull pen (no cubicles at that time), Bill said to me:

"Look, Kresge, I know that just because they're ending the GS-8 entry level, they didn't have to raise us to GS-9s, but if you'd said anything like that in his office just now, I'd have killed your ass."

I later heard the name William Barr associated with a Cabinet position, but it was perhaps a decade later before I saw Bill's picture on TV and learned how far he'd progressed while I worked as a DI analyst. How many Agency employees do you know who have been threatened with death by the future Attorney General of the United States?

www.ingramcontent.com/pod-product-compliance
Lightning Source LLC
Chambersburg PA
CBHW071618080526
44588CB00010B/1182